WITH LOVE

WITH

A Practical Guide to Caring for Aging Parents Through the End of Life

LOVE

Shari Hofer and Shabnam Kazmi

Namari Press

Published by Namari Press, Bremerton, WA
www.withloveapracticalguide.com

Edited and designed by Girl Friday Productions
www.girlfridayproductions.com

Cover design: Rachel Marek
Project management: Kim Kent
Editorial production: Kylee Hayes

ISBN (paperback): 979-8-9932089-0-9
ISBN (ebook): 979-8-9932089-1-6

Library of Congress Control Number: 2025922438

First edition

Contents

Introduction

If you have a parent or important elders in your life, you will face a moment when you realize they will not live forever. Of course, we all know that life doesn't go on forever, but death is not a reality that most of us confront head-on every day. We mostly live thinking about tomorrow, making plans for the upcoming months and years. But as parents age and become elders, their health conditions can decline. Even people who are extremely healthy start to slow down, their bodies not working quite as well as they used to. And we come face-to-face with the fact that death comes for us all eventually.

We both experienced this moment similarly, when each of our parents received medical diagnoses that made us wake up and realize that they would not be able to manage from that point to the end of their lives without some changes and support. Understanding an end-of-life journey and being able to positively cultivate it, while doing the same with your own journey in providing care, are incredibly important. Caregiving will make you face moments you cannot control, but if you are prepared and well-informed, there are many things you can influence.

If you are currently supporting an elder in some way, you

are already engaged in a caregiving journey. Many people do this without even realizing it. Are you shopping for groceries for another person? Helping them with their bills? Driving them to doctors' appointments? Sometimes caregiving grows slowly and naturally as an elder declines gradually in health and function; though, other times it can come on suddenly and dramatically due to a serious illness or injury. Regardless, many, if not all, of us will go on this journey in some way; though, we rarely think about it early enough or strategically. We face many challenges and move through the caregiving journey with potential harm to personal health, finances, career, relationships.

Going on your caregiver journey is a bit like whitewater rafting—there are many risks you can research and plan up front, but once you're on the water you have to deal with the conditions that come up, and some of them will be unexpected. Preparation makes it a successful and fulfilling experience, whereas lack of a game plan can lead to disaster. Imagine embarking on your rafting trip without knowing the difficulty of the rapids, having the right equipment, or even having a team of people to guide you. You might fall into the rapids without a helmet or life vest—not a recipe for a safe and rewarding adventure.

Similarly, your caregiving journey is most likely to have good outcomes if you make some basic decisions up front and thoughtfully assemble the tools and support that you might need. "Plan for the worst and hope for the best" is a good mindset; although, it is challenging with the uncertainties and unknowns you find in caregiving. But every bit of preparation counts and can make a world of difference.

This book approaches caregiving with that same intention, offering tools to help you feel prepared and make your caregiving journey better. What if we could think about the caregiving journey earlier and with solid insights about what makes a difference? How you prepare, engage with, and respond to all that comes up—we can all do better by having some awareness and training. Whether you are early in the process, facing challenges already, or recovering from a caregiving journey, we share insights and advice that can help you be a more effective carer for yourself, your elders, and everyone else who is on the journey with you (it's more people than you think).

We wrote this book to achieve this single goal—to positively influence your caregiving journey. We are both seasoned executives who are used to leading business ventures successfully by assessing risk and opportunity, setting a vision, creating strategic plans, leading teams, and achieving important results. We now apply those skills and experiences to reimagine what meaningful, fulfilling caregiving can look like. In this book, we share our stories of being unprepared and struggling through it all and offer reflections on what we could have done earlier to reduce stress and manage the process better. Our personal journeys provide examples and insights, while our business training applies frameworks that can help you set up structure for your own journey. Learning from each other helps us do better as individuals, and the more we talk about the challenges of caregiving, the more we can shape how companies support their employees undergoing this work and how we can show up better as spouses, friends, neighbors, colleagues. If we can help others have a less painful and challenging caregiver journey, our purpose will be met. This book is what we wish we had long before we entered some of the most challenging years of our lives.

Caregiving is complicated with a lot of uncertainties. We are not medical, eldercare, or hospice experts, and you should always consult with your healthcare teams about every step of this journey. What we can offer you is experience: We have both been through caregiving with our own parents. We both made mistakes and learned a lot along the way; we can help you approach and enter the journey with a much better idea of how to design a strategy for success. There is no one solution that will fit every situation; caregiving has too many variables. Rather, the first key to success is knowing that you need a strategy.

Navigating with a loved one to the end of their life is a topic that isn't exactly cocktail conversation. Our society tends to shy away from talking about death, thinking it is so much easier to avoid. But that is the worst thing we can do. Death is a certainty, and while much about the path is scary and uncertain, we are certainly better off raising awareness and making the dialogue around end-of-life care more comfortable and accepted—at home, in the workplace, and in the media. With an aging population and people living longer, we are all facing many more years of caregiving than ever existed in the past. How we choose to shape those years is up to us.

There is an upside to doing the hard work of planning and having a strategy for caregiving. Think of the reduction in stress, financial toxicity, broken relationships, and loss of career and identity. We can preserve so much value by doing the work early and engaging with our caregiving partners in a kind and constructive manner. Just as we plan for ventures like college or weddings, caregiving and the end of life are processes that we can plan for and shape for the better.

This book is a starting point. We don't have answers for every challenge you might face. But there are insights, lessons, and frameworks that can guide you in being a better caregiver and lead you through a more effective caregiving journey.

HOW WE GOT HERE

Before we begin, we'd like to offer you some background about our stories, how we became caregivers to our parents, how we met, why we feel so strongly about caregiving and end-of-life care, and why we wanted to write this book. We came from different backgrounds but ended up with the shared experience of caregiving that dramatically altered our lives, interjecting incredible stress and challenge but ultimately giving us strength and a whole new perspective on life. Giving meaning to this phase of our lives and channeling it for good resulted in this book, which we hope will shed light on the caregiving journey, remind those who are deep into it that they are not alone, and provide help for each stage of the journey. We bring years of education and leadership skills from our corporate careers to building this framework, filling a gap that we felt and experienced ourselves, so that you will have an easier journey yourself.

Shabnam

Every caregiver's story is unique. I was born in India, and my family immigrated to Malaysia in 1968, when I was four years old. I later moved to the United States for college when I was eighteen. My elder brother, Pervez, studied in England and later moved to Singapore, then Australia. Our younger brother, Ariff, moved to the United States and now lives in California.

My father, Syed Nasir Raza Kazmi, was a professor of English literature and worked full-time until the age of seventy-eight. He lived to ninety-two, still asking for students, as his passion was always centered on teaching. My mother, Fatiha Abbas Kazmi, was the CEO of the family and led with a big heart and bold vision. We were never wealthy and grew up away from all our family in India and Pakistan, but as immigrants in Malaysia we learned to build a new family with the people around us.

After college, I stayed and built a life in the US, becoming a citizen, marrying my husband, whom I had met in high school in Malaysia, and raising two children. My career in the pharmaceutical industry kept me traveling, and my husband's role in finance kept him busy, but we made annual visits to Malaysia almost every year from 1982 to 2020. My father passed away in 2018 and my mother in 2020. Hence, our caregiving journey involved caring for parents halfway across the globe.

Even into his late seventies, my father was active, healthy, and teaching a full course load at a university in Kuala Lumpur, where he was admired and loved. Every day he walked for an hour, and I have no memory of his ever being ill or missing a day of teaching; his asthma was manageable and he lived a simple, positive lifestyle. Then a diagnosis of Parkinson's hit in 2004 and things began to shift. The next ten years were decent, thanks to extremely good medical care by physicians such as Dr. Lee, to whom we will be forever grateful. The best medical care involved medications that controlled his disease and allowed him to live a relatively normal and functional life.

But, after that decade, the disease progressed and made walking, writing, and even swallowing difficult. My mother was a devoted and fierce caregiver for my father, but it took its toll on her, and I think she got very tired of the dreariness in the later years, as they could not socialize or travel. Dad could no longer be on a university campus. Life became lonelier and less joyous, and us children and their grandchildren brought welcome relief only once a year, at best for two or three weeks.

The more I learned about the trajectory of Parkinson's, the more I dreaded the future, but as humans do, I put those worries aside and lived appreciative of the present and what it offered. The end years were harder and more painful than I could have imagined. More awareness and preparation would have helped me navigate those years better—hence this book to help others in advance.

By the time my father passed away, it was clear that my mother had dementia. Her formal diagnosis was vascular dementia; her doctor presumed that it was caused by her cardiovascular disease, which over the years had caused too little oxygen to get to her brain. She lost function almost overnight, it seemed, although small changes had been happening for at least two years prior. That is the thing about dementia and Alzheimer's—small things start to happen that feel odd and don't make sense, and then suddenly it feels like you are looking at a completely different person. It is traumatic to experience that loss.

Since I lived in the US and my mother was in Malaysia, it took me a lot longer to figure out things were not okay with her. She was very intelligent and could quickly cover up strange things like forgetting how to do the math for paying bills and buying groceries. When you are not living with or close to an aging parent, it is important to do more than routine check-ins on the phone; being curious and aware and getting input from people around them is so important if you cannot be there in person.

My mother had full-time care at home, but my brothers and I needed to figure out who would take on more of the tasks she used to do, such as paying bills, buying groceries, making doctors' appointments, and basically organizing everything for the house and for her. When the Covid pandemic started and Malaysia shut its borders to outsiders, we had all kinds of new issues to figure out. She was incredibly sad and lonely without visitors and her children and grandchildren, and the isolation made her confused. She passed away in September 2020, and I could only attend her funeral remotely by video call. That was devastating. I felt there was no real goodbye and could not get solace from a distance.

Those tough years of loss left me completely depleted and unwell physically and emotionally. It took almost two years to feel normal again. Recovery was about regaining my physical and mental health, reestablishing my career track and new personal development goals, and finding ways to enjoy life again to the maximum. Part of the healing process was reflecting on what happened and how I could have done better. Now,

I want to use what I learned to help others in a structured way. That's why my personal goal for this book is teaching others to embrace care and own it rather than letting it own you.

Shari

It is a strange time when you realize you are switching roles with your parent or caregiver. For me, it was a slow progression, one I knew would come, though knowing that didn't make it any easier when it happened. In the back of my mind I held the thought that at some point the physical presence of my dad, whom I had become so accustomed to seeing every day, would eventually leave this earth. Now that he's gone, I know that his spirit, love, and kindness endure in my heart and consciousness forever.

I grew up in South Dakota in a small community where my parents, Joe and Bev, owned a local hardware store. I am the youngest of three: my brother, Steve, and I are sixteen years apart, while my sister, Suzanne, is three years older, so our family stretches across generations. This fact is something my parents said always kept them young at heart. Life on a prairie in the middle of the US was full of adventures, fun, and freedom. We had lots of outdoor time and spent our days exploring, swimming, and boating in summer and skiing, sledding, and snowmobiling in the winter. Autumn and spring were and still are my favorite seasons because they are the last hurrah before and after the great freeze, when the beautiful prairie state is solid ice and snow. Our lives were simple, innocent, and mostly uneventful.

When I was in high school, this changed: My mother was diagnosed with a genetic heart defect, which meant she needed a heart transplant. I became the girl with the mom who was sick in the hospital hours away in Minneapolis, Minnesota. With her new heart, we did get a tremendous gift of twelve extra years, but she was always on a timeline. Still, when my mother passed away in 1999, it seemed far too soon.

I had just turned twenty-eight, was recently married to my first husband, and we were living in Chicago. I had made the decision to hold off on law school to join the internet boom, and life was moving fast and furious, both exhilarating and exhausting. My mom's death hit me like a Mack truck. The grief was profound, no match for the anguish about her illness that I had been carrying concealed for years. I had so many plans for events that I wanted her to see and be part of. I wasn't ready to say goodbye, but life doesn't work that way and our time together in this life was ending. Mom was the rock of our family, the graceful presence that kept us all in line. When she passed away, it became clear to my sister, brother, and me that our dad would need help.

What we did not know was that my father was already in the early stages of dementia, and in about fourteen years—I was in my second marriage, had two children, some career change, and a few global moves—we would be moving him across the country, out of South Dakota to Washington, where we were living, to be close to us so we could help take care of him. For me, this was ideal—not the dementia, of course, but having my dad close by, mostly so my kids could get to know him better. He was Papa Joe or just Papa to all the grandkids. We had already lived in amazing places like California, Italy, and Hawaii, but we were never near family. So having my dad move close to us and my sister, who was about one hour away, was like a dream come true.

While the closeness was great, I did not get much time to appreciate it because I was just trying to survive. Between my career, raising my kids, taking care of our household, and caregiving for my father, I had a lot going on. It wasn't until after he was gone that I could look back and appreciate all we had. It is hard to explain, but when you lose a parent, it is like a piece of you just vanishes one day. Their physical presence is gone, but their spirit, mannerisms, and approach to life remain within you and your family.

This is my story about caregiving for my dad through his journey with dementia. It is my truth, a bit raw and abbreviated at times but authentic.

Shabnam and I hope our stories can help you understand you are not alone in this beautiful and oftentimes unpredictable journey. And our hope is that something in our stories will help you in your journey. We are driven to elevate caregiving as a conversation we should all be thinking about and planning for.

HOW TO USE THIS BOOK

This book is organized into three major parts according to each stage of caregiving. Within each chapter you will find a description of the issue we are providing guidance on, our stories and personal experiences that shaped our journeys, and our insights and advice to enhance your journey. Here is a basic overview.

Part One: Making Key Decisions

Setting the stage for effective caregiving ideally starts before there is any major health condition requiring a change in living arrangements or support. This is a great time to lay the foundation for care, with an overall strategy and proactive planning.

- Chapter 1: Healthcare and Medical Factors— Understand current healthcare needs and plan for future ones.
- Chapter 2: Legal and Financial Planning—Prepare necessary paperwork and gain an understanding of the health of the financial affairs.
- Chapter 3: The Place of Care—Understand the different living options so you can determine a best fit.

Part Two: The Caregiving Life

This section is for when care management steps up and declining health no longer allows for independent living or minimal support. Hospitalizations, injuries, and declining mental and physical functioning necessitate greater support from caregivers. This can be an intensive period of caregiving that lasts a long time and requires heavy resources.

- Chapter 4: Assembling and Managing Care— Coordinate support services from professionals, family, and friends.

- Chapter 5: Self-Caregiving—How to take care of yourself along the way.
- Chapter 6: Managing Career and Caregiving— Navigating work along with caregiving responsibilities.

Part Three: Facing the Inevitable and Moving Forward

Even with care there is a natural end to life, and here we discuss all that comes with losing a loved one. Dealing with death, working through grief, and resetting oneself to be able to move forward toward a new normal all takes work as well.

- Chapter 7: Approaching the Final Destination— Recognize signs, honor wishes, and prepare for the death of your loved one.
- Chapter 8: The Moment of Death—What happens when the moment comes, and what needs to happen after.
- Chapter 9: Making Peace and Moving Forward— Healing and finding the new normal.

We shared many aspects of our caregiving journeys in common, such as our close and loving families, active and high-pressure career tracks, financial flexibility, and a high commitment to doing the utmost for loved ones. But we also have some differences in the constraints and challenges we faced, such as geographic distance, cultural norms, range and cost of resources available to us for caregiving, and others. Throughout the book we generally use *parents* or *loved one* to refer to the elder persons we are caregiving, but the information in this book is applicable no matter your relationship or the specifics of your situation.

So this book allows us to bring both our stories and those of others together for a wide range of perspectives that we believe can inform and educate anyone who is currently on this journey. Like the travelers who used the stars to navigate, you don't have to start from scratch. Knowledge that is gained, organized, and shared can provide a compass (and GPS!) to ease your journey and save you from pitfalls.

We both come from a position of education, financial resources, strong family and community support, and job skills. This happened to be our fortunate position when we entered our caregiving journeys, and yet we struggled greatly. We hope that this book will prove helpful no matter what circumstances you have before and after your own journey.

We also bring a heavily female-oriented perspective because of who we are, but in researching for this book and engaging with hundreds of people, we have been moved by the range of caregivers themselves. Men are taking significantly bigger roles and are also often primary caregivers, the demographic is younger (sometimes much younger) than we were and sometimes as young as in their teens and early adulthood, and there is every version of family situation, such as people taking care of their in-laws, aunts, and even neighbors. We believe there are useful lessons in this book for most everyone in some way.

At the end of the book are resources that can help you dig deeper into each of the topics covered and a curated list to assist you, as there is too much information on the internet.

PART ONE

Making Key Decisions

1

Healthcare and Medical Factors

Health is not a given. When we are relatively healthy and able-bodied, this is not something we always think about. But health conditions change, and our caregiving journey is shaped significantly by the health of the loved ones we are caring for. Whether it is a chronic condition, an acute health problem, or a combination of the two, a shift happens when the status quo is no longer possible and actions have to be taken. For some, it may be a catastrophic diagnosis like cancer; for others, it may be a progression of dementia, cardiovascular disease, or diabetes. The nature of the health condition sets into motion a whole lot of questions, including assumptions around prognosis, timing, and the likely care requirements ahead.

The truth is that preparing for caregiving is no longer a should-do but a must-do. With the skyrocketing cost of healthcare and the number of Americans over the age of sixty-five set to double, the majority of us will be affected. Making the shift to parenting our parents or caregiving for a spouse, child, or friend is challenging work. The best way to begin your caregiving journey is to start making plans before your loved one needs care. If you're already past that point, though—don't worry! This chapter is your starting place no matter where your loved one is on their journey.

So we begin with getting a lay of the land, which includes an understanding of conditions, healthcare management decisions, and payment considerations. You will wear many hats along the way, so be prepared. We were schedulers, advocates, interpreters, question askers, rule followers, and so much more. This chapter outlines some of the first things you will likely encounter, and we'll explore them together so you know what you need to do to be prepared:

- Understanding medical conditions and treatment options
- Confirming insurance coverage
- Having open discussions with parents and family

UNDERSTANDING MEDICAL CONDITIONS AND TREATMENT OPTIONS

Shari

Healthcare can be a sticky subject, and it's not always one that parents want to share with their children. What makes this even more challenging is that you are dealing with someone who is aging, in most cases, or even ill. This adds another layer of complexity, as many do not want to openly discuss their decline or admit they need to stop doing things. However, in order to be an effective caregiver, you need to have a good understanding of what you are dealing with so you can manage it. It took us a while to really understand what we were dealing with regarding my dad's dementia. Once we understood it, everything made much more sense, but to get to this point it required a lot of questions, powers of attorney, research, and some difficult truth telling.

My dad was born in the 1920s and was part of what is called the Greatest Generation, or the GI Generation. He and a group of his friends enlisted in the US Navy right after Pearl Harbor, while he was a senior in high school. A few weeks after graduation, he was on a train bound for Naval Station Great Lakes. My dad was kind, charismatic, and curious. He prided himself on having only one hospital stay after breaking his arm by falling off a horse in eighth grade. And at ninety-four, he took one medication daily and that was it. He lived his life half full, and his mantra was "Every day is a good day." I know this mindset had everything to do with his longevity. He was 100 percent Irish and loved telling stories and jokes. He was an incredible man and father. One thing he did not love, though—and even avoided with great vigor—was going to the doctor.

As my dad's health started to decline, our involvement in his healthcare became essential. The bottom line was my dad did not want to talk about his health, and although he went to the doctor, it was only after much suffering. He was most happy saying goodbye to the doctor as he walked out the door. This was not because he didn't respect doctors or their practice—doctors had saved my mother's and my niece's lives—but he was just not interested in hearing or talking about himself.

If you have a parent or are caregiving for someone from this generation, I feel for you. It is best to understand that you may be the one setting up appointments or even attending them with your parent. But if that is not an option, be sure that you set up a direct line of communication with healthcare providers and receive updates from them promptly. You must be prudent about listening and following through, because your parent may not do it, for a variety of reasons. My dad was humble to a fault, and he would rather hear about other people than talk about himself. He was just glad to be alive and cherished every moment. But this meant I couldn't get the clearest or most up-to-date information about his health straight from the horse's mouth. So we were always on a mining exercise for the true state of my father's health until we finally got to meet with his doctor. After that, it was clear to us that my dad was legally blind due to macular degeneration, had dementia, and was suffering from untreated osteoarthritis in his knees that was affecting his ability to walk.

There had been several recommendations from the doctor that my father just frankly ignored. For example, the osteoarthritis in his knees made falling a huge risk. So he had received a cane and then a walker from Veterans Affairs (the VA), both of which sat idle in the basement of his home. Getting him to use these was a daily challenge; however, the threat of breaking something and having to be in the hospital eventually won out and he started to reluctantly use them. Once he got used to the walker, I think he actually liked it. He could move faster and freer than before, but getting there was a battle.

Once a diagnosis is made, it is your job to become as much of an expert as possible in that condition. For me, this involved lots of research and asking the doctor lots of questions. This is also when it becomes critical to understand the type of doctor you are going to and why. Our general practitioner was his main doctor for some time, and while helpful, they were clear that they were not experts on dementia and geriatric care. They were always willing to help, but their help was often limited and they often didn't have answers when it came to specific questions.

My recommendation is to make sure you have access to a neurologist or a specialist for your loved one's specific needs. If a general practitioner is still the main doctor your loved one is seeing, make sure they have some familiarity with geriatric care. You can also find a lot of information for yourself online, but whatever information you find should always be vetted by a doctor who knows the specifics of your loved one's case and condition. I tried to focus on using primary sources, peer-reviewed research, or society websites. While I found information about dementia all over the internet, most of it was not deep enough to help. Support groups, either online or in person, for people going through the same thing can also be a great educational resource.

Shabnam

When a parent gets à new medical diagnosis, it sets off a chain of events that can quickly overwhelm you. First comes assessing of the problem, then comes solving it; this can take a lot of time and effort, especially if the condition is uncommon or complex. Whether it's serious, urgent, or unexpected; has long-term or short-term implications; or entails a set of treatment and management requirements, every diagnosis requires a plan of action.

A great place to start is with the healthcare professionals closest to your parent, but that is only the beginning. You may want to seek second opinions, see other associated and relevant specialists, and learn from online resources and people who may have experienced the same situation. Also remember that medical conditions don't necessarily get taken care of easily or quickly. It is best to approach challenges with calm and a spirit of strength, remembering that you can be most effective if you don't panic and become overwhelmed. Lean on those you can trust for support, and use all the resources that are available to you. There's no need to reinvent the wheel!

On a routine visit, my father's neurologist, Dr. Lee, noticed something was not right with Mum. Her keen eyes and expertise picked up signs of something we had not understood, although the signs had been there in various ways. Dr. Lee had experienced many years of Mum's command of Dad's healthcare, her sharp wit and intelligence (is "tiger wife" a thing?). I noticed the concern in Dr. Lee's eyes when she said, "Let's get you a scan, Mrs. Kazmi." Confused and panicked, I waited for her assessment of the scan, already somehow knowing it would not be good.

"Your mother's brain has shrunk to the size of an apple," Dr. Lee said as she showed me the scan, revealing a strangely small brain with dark patches everywhere, hardly like the ones you see in the media. I was speechless, unable to ask what this meant for her, for us, but suddenly everything made sense. I thought about the odd things that had begun showing up about two years prior, like getting phone calls at 3:00 a.m. I never turned off my cell phone—I was the primary caregiver and needed to be accessible for my parents and my children no matter what time zone I was in or what time it was. So picking up a call at 3:00 a.m. always spiked my heart rate: *Something is really wrong,* I'd think. But several times it was just Mum being social and calling to chat. That made no sense, and she'd get embarrassed, asking for a clock that would show both US and Malaysian time side by side. But it is a twelve-hour time difference, so I would say, "Mum, if it is three in the afternoon for you, it is three in the morning for me. Easy enough, right?" Little did I realize her brain could no longer do that simple math or logic.

Next she lost the ability to manage cash, handing people 500 ringgit (about US$117) in exchange for groceries worth perhaps 25 ringgit (about $6). Her helpers, Pushpa and Melissa, had been in-home carers for several years, so they'd noticed the changes in Mum's behaviors, although they did not understand why she was behaving differently. Gradual changes are hard to pick up and understand without a formal diagnosis of dementia.

Mum resented the implication that she was doing anything

wrong or strange. When we ultimately took away her check-book and cash, she was angry and depressed. It was painful to see someone who had been competent and in charge all her life lose the functional abilities that had been a big part of her identity.

Once we got her diagnosis, it was all about getting the right treatments in place and figuring out how to shift responsibility for all the things she couldn't handle to others. Treatment was a huge challenge because there aren't good drugs or approaches for managing dementia and every patient has to be titrated to a regimen that will work with them to manage symptoms such as anxiety, depression, or aggressiveness.

The first medication my mother received caused such hallucinations that neighbors would get concerned and come check on her. They heard her shouting loudly, which was very uncharacteristic, as she was usually confident and controlled. Since the apartments were close by and neighbors quite social, they worried when they heard her sounding frantic and angry, unlike her usual cheerful self. It was a harrowing time for the helpers who were taking care of my mother, as they did not have experience with the illness and all the behavior changes that can ensue. After multiple rounds of different medications, we were finally able to find a combination that allowed Mum to be calm, peaceful, and eventually happy and able to enjoy a decent quality of life in the comfort of her own home.

CONFIRMING INSURANCE COVERAGE

Health insurance coverage in the United States can be one of the trickiest and most time-consuming activities for caregivers to figure out. The first thing to understand is whether your loved one is carrying coverage—if they are using VA benefits, Medicare, Medicaid, Social Security, a retirement pension plan, private insurance coverage, or marketplaces—or if they are uninsured and pay cash for healthcare. The eligibility requirements vary, but here's a quick summary: VA is only available to those who've served in the US Armed Forces. When you turn sixty-five in the US, you are eligible for Medicare as long as you or your spouse have paid Medicare taxes for at least ten years or forty quarters (every year has four quarters in it). You also need to be a US citizen or legal resident to be eligible and have lived in the US for five continuous years. Once you meet these requirements, you are eligible for premium-free Medicare, which is known as Part A.

If someone is on Social Security or a Railroad Retirement Board benefit for at least four months prior to their sixty-fifth birthday, they are automatically enrolled in Medicare Parts A and D. If those don't apply, then there is a seven-month window around the sixty-fifth birthday in which they have to enroll in Medicare. Give yourself plenty of time for filing and be prepared to hurry up and wait. If these requirements are not met, they can still get Medicare Part B, which requires a premium.

As with everything, there is nuance and a lot of rules, so read very carefully and know the specifics for the state in which your loved one lives. Most importantly, don't forget to apply if you need it. Not having coverage on time is like trying to nail Jell-O to a wall. In addition, it is one thing to have the coverage and another to understand what it actually covers.

Shari's dad had VA benefits, so they used that for everything. It has pluses and minuses, as do all federally or state-funded healthcare choices. Just do your research and stay on top of it, because regulations change frequently.

Shari

When I look at photos of my dad over the years, I see the decline in pictures, but I am unsure if I saw—or perhaps chose not to see—the decline at the time. It felt like he was just aging. Then he fell. The decline after this event was so rapid that we never got to utilize my dad's long-term care policy. This is additional insurance you can buy specifically to be used when a person can no longer perform daily activities. It typically covers some, if not all, of the cost of one-to-one care either at home or in an assisted living facility. If your parent or elder has this insurance, make sure you understand its terms, how to activate it, and any limits it may have. In some states, it is mandatory to add money to a state-funded long-term care policy. In some cases, this is funded by a payroll tax and has a cap, so check with your state.

My dad's long-term care insurance was something that he prided himself on purchasing with my mother when they were younger so that their children wouldn't need to worry about them. His policy only covered one-to-one care, not senior apartments like the one we ended up choosing for him. And many of these policies have minimum thresholds that you must meet for them to kick in, such as the person cannot walk unassisted or eat without assistance. The typical minimum threshold is three criteria, but unfortunately my dad's was four. It also had a cap on the number of years you could use it. For example, if the cap is five years, that means that after five years, whether you need it longer or not, the insurance stops paying. When we were not able to activate the plan due to his condition not fitting the strict requirements, it meant we paid for his care and living arrangements out of pocket.

We did not share with him that we could not use the long-term care plan; frankly, at that point, I am not sure he would have fully understood that, and it would have only upset him. A part of him was wrapped up in that idea of "never being a burden" to anyone—those are the words he used. He didn't want us to have to pay for his living expenses because, in most cases, health insurance does not cover the cost of care facilities. This can differ for Medicaid or skilled nursing facilities, so be sure you understand the type of coverage and read the policies very carefully to know what healthcare is covered and whether there is a long-term care policy.

Having a good understanding of a long-term care policy will free up much of your headspace to focus on caregiving.

HAVING OPEN DISCUSSIONS WITH PARENTS AND FAMILY

Depending on where you are in the journey, the big step is to start having hard conversations and asking questions. Being able to understand your loved one's wishes and knowing their limits and non-negotiables is critical when caregiving. It removes the pressure from making all the decisions yourself and helps when you have to make very difficult choices. Knowing that you are fulfilling their wishes also carries forward the dignity and respect that they deserve.

Communication is critical to success with caregiving. It can be conversations with the one you are caring for, siblings, medical professionals, and other caregivers who may be helping you. Start with the one you are caring for. Have an open and honest conversation about where they are in their health and life journey and what their wishes are for the future. This is where you can uncover how they feel about options such as leaving their home and moving into a more structured care facility. These conversations can be tough with parents for a number of reasons, but having them early gives you time to plan for the future. Timing and state of health often play a role in these conversations as well.

When you are having these discussions, here are a few foundational questions for you to consider, starting with:

1. What is my loved one's understanding of their health?
2. What is the true state of my loved one's health? Do they have a diagnosis? What meds are they taking and why?
3. What are their preferences if their health gets worse and they need more care? Do they want to be at home or in a care facility? What don't they want? What compromises are they willing to make?

4. What are your preferences (or those of other
   potential caregivers)? How are you able to contribute to their care?

Answering these questions will give you a solid understanding of how to build a plan that fulfills your loved one's
requirements. Of course, there may be some compromising
needed or unexpected changes that come up, but it will help
you to know that you can make decisions with their interest
and wishes in mind.

In order to facilitate difficult conversations, it is helpful to
find a comfortable setting away from the distractions of daily
life. Creating an environment that is peaceful and relaxed,
even bringing a little humor into the setting, can be helpful.
Depending on the family dynamics, making the conversation
more structured or formal may be useful; regardless, try to
gear the setting of the discussion to suit your audience.

Take a sensitive approach; these are your parents after
all, and they deserve kindness and respect. Imagine yourself
in their shoes: How would you want to work through the important questions and decision-making? Empathy goes a long
way in getting to productive dialogue. It is also important to
have some goals and not leave things too open-ended. Once
the conversation begins, start with understanding. Ask a lot
of questions and don't assume you know your parents' wishes;
you might be surprised by what's most important to them. It is
also important to keep a curious and open mind as you start to
build scenarios and options together. Ask "what if" questions
such as "What if you were to move closer to us?" or "What if
we are all in different parts of the country and you chose to

stay in place, how could we set up things to work?" These kinds of questions open up discussion rather than promoting simple yes or no responses.

Sometimes, when parents are unable to make decisions for themselves, their children or caregivers have to take the lead. For example, when cognitive reasoning declines, there is a point at which it is obvious that they will not be able to remain in place. This is an extremely difficult situation and ideally you have already put in the legal paperwork to be able to assume their care on their behalf. But this doesn't happen overnight, and there is often resistance to change; being firm, kind, and practical is important to avoid negative situations.

Don't try to solve everything all at once; complex and important decisions take time to think through and align multiple parties around. Start the dialogue, take a pause if necessary, and come back to it when there is a chance to progress. Learning from others' experiences helps, as does sharing stories of how friends and others successfully created good working arrangements. Everyone involved in these decisions is vulnerable, and we are all trying to come up with a solution that works best for everyone.

Acknowledging early on that any options on the table will require the associated funding is also important. Having a rough sense of costs, as you would when buying a car or a house, is a basic starting point. In a sense, you are shopping for the ideal solution that you can afford. Money, however, is a really hard part of the end-of-life dialogue, no matter how much is available. It raises all kinds of insecurities and creates tensions across the people involved, as it is tied to control and freedom and independence and choice.

Establishing a common goal, such as maximizing the resources available and matching them up to what is desired for
care, can also benefit from building scenarios. What if they
live to eighty? Ninety? Beyond? What if intensive care is required? Sometimes the best case of living longer can become
the worst case of requiring expensive, long-term, high-level
care—what then? More financial services firms are providing
guidance to their clients on these issues.

Shari

My caregiving journey technically started in my early forties
with two school-age children, a full-time global job requiring
travel, and an active-duty military spouse who was frequently
away. Actually, to be honest and fair to myself, the journey really started at fifteen when my mom was sick, and it went on
for years. But when I started caregiving for my dad, he was
in his eighties and lived several states away from us, in South
Dakota. While my siblings and I knew my dad was aging, we
didn't yet know the extent of his health problems, which included increasing dementia, legal blindness, and mobility issues. We mostly asked the right questions, and he was open
about his financial status and life insurance policies.

Still, the bottom line was that he did not have much money
left after paying for my mother's care, and he lived on a very
fixed income. In his mind, he had a plan that included a small
life insurance policy, Social Security, healthcare from the VA,
and the long-term care insurance policy. It was a plan, but it
mainly existed in his mind and didn't factor in realities such

as: we all lived in different states, the current health situation he was facing, and his lack of proactivity around his issues.

From our perspective, he was slowly entering a time when he needed to be in an environment that could offer care. Also, we did not want him to be so far away, so we started planning and strategizing. If you are at this point and can do some planning beforehand, I highly recommend it. It will save you and your family lots of stress. If I could do it all over again, I would have done more up front rather than trying to figure it out when things were already in motion.

In his moments of clarity, my dad would talk about how he knew his ability to take care of himself was diminishing, but he did not want to plan any changes to his lifestyle. So this meant we needed to do it for him. At other times, he seemed unaware that he was having issues. Having these conversations is both an art and a skill, and I tried to find ways to work in a discussion of health, as my dad mostly did not want to talk about it. As the conversations evolved, I often felt compelled to exercise my people-pleasing nature. I would ask tough questions but not rock the boat too much, attempting to drop subtle hints as we went along. The first challenge we faced was where he was going to live. No matter what kind of care situation he ended up with, we were already planning to move Dad from South Dakota to Washington so he'd be closer to us. The problem? I knew it was going to be an argument.

It was August in South Dakota, a particularly stuffy time. Gone were the sweet green days of June and July, and upon us was the humid end of summer and prep for autumn. My dad's birthday was coming up and his driver's license needed to be renewed. His plan was not to renew it since his eyesight had gotten so bad. Along with his eyesight, we would later learn that his dementia was progressing.

Dementia is not a smooth, linear journey. There were good and bad days, times when things were going fine and times we noticed things that weren't quite right about his behavior or memory. It is a terrible disease and hard to fully connect the dots when you are so far away, but when we were with my dad, we could see and experience these changes. It was apparent his health was declining.

By this point, we had been dropping hints about the potential move for months, though it was clear he was not going to come willingly. Every time we brought it up, he got very agitated and acted like it wasn't something we'd discussed at all before. Then Dad's birthday rolled around and he showed up at the driver's license office despite telling us he would not. This behavior of lying or changing his plans last minute was becoming a habit, just another one of those indicators that all was not well. After a few failures on the eye exam, they renewed his license for another year. How? I felt so let down by the system for many reasons, but mostly it stung because it meant that we would have to step up and let my dad know he would not be driving anymore. It simply wasn't safe for him or the other drivers on the road.

I, along with my siblings, confronted Dad about the license, his last-minute change of plan, and the fact that he should not be driving. Of course, not having a license is one of the more challenging things for the aging because it limits their freedom. In his best dad voice, he assured me the driver's license was merely for identification purposes, and he would not be driving. I really wanted to believe him. But I'd dearly loved and cherished this man for all my life, and I knew he fully intended to continue driving.

At this point, it was highly likely that this and other conversations we'd had with him would be forgotten, and if he needed to go somewhere, he would jump in the car and go like he always did. In addition, I am sure being told over the phone what to do by your youngest daughter, who lived in another part of the country, did not carry much weight. I was still the little girl who wanted my dad to agree with me, see me, and do everything we'd agreed on. But more than anything, I was worried about his safety. We rallied and pushed forward with the plan to move my dad out of South Dakota. We all knew the universe was testing us with the driver's license and, sooner or later, he was going to hurt himself or someone else.

If I had the chance to do it again, I would just tell him that his having a license in his condition was not safe and he needed to be close to his family. Rather than dragging it out over months of dropping comments and hints and then feeling frustrated that he just wouldn't get with the program, I would have just told him the truth. That conversation would have been complicated, and it was hard when we finally did it, but directness mixed with kindness is the best way.

Shabnam

Shortly after my dad's Parkinson's diagnosis, we realized he should not be driving to the university, as it was unsafe for him and others. His reflexes were declining, and we could see from his walk that he was shuffling his feet and taking longer to get around. Often his hands would shake, and their strength started to decline as well. We suggested he should not drive, but my father was adamant that he could. It was his means to get to his job and his passion, which was the university. It was a topic we did not want to push, because the implication was so negative for my father. Who was he if he didn't teach? We would bring up the topic and then quickly exit the discussion because none of us wanted to be the one to take away the last form of independence and joy from my father.

Eventually, Mum and I decided to sell the car—it was the only way to make the break. We did not fully realize the psychological impact of taking away Dad's freedom, his teaching, and his students. I still wonder if we could have done something like hire a driver to take him back and forth to the university, anything that could have given my father more time with his teaching, independence, and joy. We might have managed for a while, but the reality is that the time for that difficult decision would still have come.

It is really hard to make tough decisions. It is really hard to be the bad guy. But making your loved one's safety a priority has to be done sometimes, so don't delay or avoid decisions like these. People respect having a clear conversation that is objective and practical. We made the decision for my dad, but instead we should have persuaded him to own the decision and buy into it himself. Cutting him out of the decision made him resentful, sad, and powerless; this is not good for the psyche. I recommend you try to include your parent in the decision-making, even for the difficult choices.

Even a decade later, when I asked Dad if there was anything I could do for him, he said, "Bring me students." It broke my heart. By then he could not write, he could barely read, and the Kindle, books, and computer that used to follow him everywhere in the house were left untouched, although books had to always be within reach. At the end, I could barely make out his voice from the impact of the disease.

While these conversations can be challenging, they are foundational in creating a plan that you can follow before you reach a point of crisis or a point at which your loved one cannot participate in the decision-making process.

Ask Yourself

- Do I understand my loved one's condition and the treatment options available? If not, who can clarify that for me?
- Does my loved one understand their health condition?
- What is my loved one's insurance coverage? How much money will the treatment require and where will it come from?
- Who will be on the caregiving team? Whom can I ask for help?
- How can I support my loved one, and what do I need to change at home or work to enable this?

Ask Your Loved One

- What are your goals if your health worsens?
- What are your fears?

- What trade-offs are you willing to make or not willing to make?
- What is most important to you as we think about the end of life?
- What are your wishes?

CHAPTER TAKEAWAYS

The caregiving journey often begins with a significant health condition being identified for a parent or loved one. This condition is usually one that is major enough to signal that things will look different going forward. Something changes in the functioning and independence of the parent, and everything shifts. This can be a gradual change in daily living or a sudden change in cases of acute or catastrophic medical conditions.

And this is where your role as caregiver becomes crystallized, as the situation requires you to take on a new set of responsibilities that you did not anticipate previously. It is a pivotal moment in time, as you have to decide how much of yourself you can throw into caregiving, how you will share responsibilities with others, and what the scope of work is that will need to be managed. Things will change, of course: The healthcare outlook can become better or worse over time, you will have ups and downs as you navigate through the caregiving journey, and you will learn and adapt.

To reduce stress for yourself and your loved ones, be sure to take the time to understand medical conditions and treatment options, confirm insurance coverage, and have open discussions with everyone involved. This will pay off in the long run and influence your caregiving experience significantly. Make sure you do your own research on the types of insurance coverage and understand long-term care. Specifically, it is important to note that every policy is different, and many do not cover vision or dental care. This means that even if you are able to take advantage of care options, you may still be paying out of pocket for vision or dental issues. While we have offered some baseline information in this chapter, every state has different rules and every policy has different guidelines, so it is best to review them to be sure.

2

Legal and Financial Planning

A key area to start mapping early in the caregiving journey is legal and financial planning. It is essential to be very clear we are not giving legal advice here, as we are not qualified to do so; what we provide is a framework for planning and an understanding of how and why this is important to tackle.

Legal planning allows the various stakeholders to have their rights and wishes aligned with the process and actions that will be required and assigns the power to make decisions clearly to certain individuals. For example, if a senior is no longer able to make decisions on their own due to dementia or other cognitive decline, there needs to be a clearly identified responsible person who can make decisions for them. The same goes for assets; it needs to be clear what assets exist, how they should be used, and who has the power to make those choices.

Financial planning and legal planning overlap, but financial planning is more tactical in identifying what funds are available—both owned by the seniors and to be contributed by family members—and modeling scenarios for what different types of care may cost (what level of care and how long, acute versus chronic care, in-home versus formal). Since there are so many uncertainties, and the topic involves facing difficult things about aging and losing health, we tend to avoid addressing the important benefits of doing this planning.

Retirement planning is often inadequate, and we need better tools to model various scenarios and see how assumptions can affect outcomes. This chapter provides some insights and learnings based on our experiences. If nothing else—put this on your priority list for yourself and your elders! You will save yourself much heartache later on and come out of the journey in much better shape if you make even simple plans together.

Getting professional help to build out your legal and financial plans is an excellent idea because these things are complicated and laws are different in each state and country. Unless the right paperwork is filed in the right way, it could be meaningless when needed. Without proper legal documentation, important decisions will be made by the state and federal governments.

LEGAL CONSIDERATIONS

There are many legal issues to consider when caregiving, and each state has different laws and expectations, so take everything you read as something you need to investigate further. For example, if you plan to relocate your parent to another state, all their documents will need to be reviewed and revised in the new state. Here are the key things to consider:

- Find a reputable elder law attorney and understand state laws.
- Obtain advance directives and power of attorney (POA) for healthcare, durable POA, additional POA for potential capacity issues, and advance directives.
- Review and update wills.

Find an Elder Law Attorney

The first step is to locate a reputable attorney who is knowledgeable about the laws of your state (or the state where your loved one resides) and specifically works with elder law. Many people think that an estate attorney is enough, but these types of lawyers do not do the same work.

A good rule of thumb is that elder law attorneys focus on the legal needs of seniors while they are alive and estate attorneys focus on asset distribution after death. Estate attorneys typically don't have the scope of knowledge that elder law attorneys have on Medicare, Medicaid, long-term care, and incapacity planning. Most elder law attorneys can help with basic estate planning, powers of attorney, healthcare directives, guardianship, and elder abuse and exploitation. Be sure to take your time to find an attorney who can help with the unique requirements of your situation.

Obtain Advance Directives

When stepping into this role as a caregiver, you need to first decide on durable power of attorney for healthcare, and a more specific one, depending on the conditions and laws of the state where your parent resides.

First, let's talk about what these terms mean. A power of attorney is a document in which you can appoint an agent or attorney-in-fact to operate on your behalf. The limitation here is that if you become incapacitated, a general POA is no longer valid. This is why a durable POA is the better option, as it appoints someone you trust to manage your financial and healthcare decisions when you cannot. It is important to note that both documents expire upon death of the principal (the person whom the document is about).

The requirements for a POA, or durable POA, will vary from state to state, so be sure that if you are living in a different state from a parent and traveling back and forth, your documentation is good for the state where your parent resides. We can't stress the importance of this document enough if you are caregiving for a dementia patient or anyone facing a long-term illness where they will need help at some point with their affairs and making decisions.

There are several types of POAs, so be very clear what you want and make sure you understand what is covered. Some states are very protective of elders and concerned about people taking advantage of them in declining conditions, so getting this done early is very helpful. It is also good to verify if some states require a separate POA for financial affairs or for potential capacity issues.

The next item of importance is the living will, which is a type of advance directive specifying medical treatment preferences, including life-sustaining measures. Advance directives lay out the wishes for medical care if you become incapacitated. If someone cannot communicate their preferences at the time that medical or emergency intervention is necessary, this document helps to do that and should cover resuscitation, mechanical ventilation, and artificial treatment. It's important to note that the living will is different from a will, which we'll discuss next.

When you have both, it allows you to fulfill the wishes of the person you are caregiving for specifically. Your loved one's healthcare providers or hospice will also require these documents and can help you get them in some cases. It is the best way to make sure you are abiding by the wishes of the person you are caregiving for.

Review and Update Wills

Having a will and keeping it updated is a critical component to settling estates. If there is not a will when a person passes away, it is considered dying intestate and the assets are distributed following the intestate laws of the state of residence, which can be time- and money-consuming. Having a legally binding will also allows you or your loved one to choose an estate administrator. Some assets, such as a life insurance policy, can bypass this process if they were assigned beneficiaries. Without a will, in many cases the estate will go into the probate process, which can be long and stressful. If there are assets involved, it is best to have a will completed, and the elder law attorney can help with this as well. In a case where there are no assets or assets have been liquidated, this may not be an issue.

Shari

After my mother passed away, my dad did not keep the will up to date. We made plans to liquidate most of his assets when we moved him to Washington, so at the time of his death he did not have assets under his name; it worked out okay for us.

My mother-in-law's situation was very different. We lost her in a very unexpected and untimely way. She had been caring for her husband, who was very ill, and had him in a skilled nursing facility while she prepared for an outpatient procedure of her own. While the procedure was successful, she passed away in her sleep following it. Without a will in the state where they lived, all her assets went to the husband. While things were eventually settled, it took much from both sides of the family; there were accusations, heartache, and hurt to get there. The point is that having a will can help you avoid these circumstances, while making sure the wishes of your loved one are carried out in a thoughtful and caring way.

FINANCIAL PLANNING

As with legal documentation, making sure to have financial affairs in order is critical, and if you can do it early on you will have fewer issues to deal with along the way, and especially when your loved one passes. Here are the basics:

- Obtain POA for financial matters.
- Develop a plan for managing assets.
- Consider the tax implications of claiming an elder as a dependent.

Obtain Financial POA

As mentioned in the previous section, in many cases a separate POA is needed specifically for finances. Make sure your POA is specific enough to address how financial matters will be handled before and when there is a loss of capacity as well as after death. If you have a durable POA, be sure to consult an elder law or estate attorney where your loved one resides to make sure it is sufficient for financial matters.

Develop an Asset Management Plan

Once the financial POA is in place (see previous section), it is time to start understanding assets and liabilities and building a plan to manage them. Locate all accounts, make sure you can easily access them, and assess the financial situation. All accounts that have assets in them are payable upon death; this includes joint checking and saving accounts. If you do not have election on your accounts, it can take months to access accounts, even if your name is on them or you have a financial POA.

It is also wise to check whether to set up joint accounts. There are mixed recommendations on this matter, and it is best to understand this before you move forward with adding yourself or siblings to your parents' accounts. Check with the bank to understand their policies. It is also very important to look into credit cards, automatic payments, and terms for both of these. Over the years, seniors have been vulnerable to various scams and can find themselves in precarious situations when it comes to credit card fraud, so it is best to close accounts wherever possible and monitor all activity on open accounts.

One recommendation is to set up a limited liability company (LLC) to manage the affairs and estate. This can help simplify management by assigning it to a trusted adult child or fiduciary who can handle paying the bills and making decisions. It avoids the possibility of a court-appointed conservatorship or guardian. The manager can control how and where the funds go, so you can make sure funds are used appropriately. It also provides legal liability protection and ensures privacy. Ultimately, an LLC protects those you are caregiving for as well as yourself from any nefarious activity.

When and if you take over financials, it is wise to make sure you have any and all passwords for phones, email accounts, social media accounts, and other apps. As a business practice, social media and phone companies are difficult if not impossible to work with in these situations and often will not provide the passwords. There are password management apps that can be useful for saving and sharing this information securely.

Shari

When we got access to my dad's financials, we started to see more evidence that there was an issue with his cognition. Somehow, he had managed to sign up for several credit cards. He had only charged on one card but had signed up for balance protection services on all of them. This means a monthly service fee is charged to help protect the user should they lose a job or source of income and not be able to pay their credit card bills on time. These fees meant my dad had a total balance of over $20,000. He could not see well and would send a minimum monthly payment, but he did not compute that his balance was growing even though he was not actively charging. Thousands of seniors in the US fell prey to this scam. All the major credit card companies were doing this, and eventually they had to stop. In the end, my brother-in-law was able to get a portion of the fees taken off for my dad and we paid the remainder.

My dad was never aggressive or angry, which can happen with some folks with dementia. However, he grew increasingly stressed about money, mainly how much things cost and who paid for them. I believe it stemmed from my dad's concern about being a burden and a scarcity mindset imprinted on him in childhood, not something uncommon for those raised during the Depression. He did not want to be seen or thought of as the person causing financial distress and did not want his children to pay for anything to support him.

When this subject came up, it was often in the evening, when his sundown syndrome showed up. *Sundowning* is a term used when someone with dementia starts displaying more confusion in the evenings. They often pick a topic and really drill into it, or become very focused on it. Since the topic of money generally caused distress in my father, I would typically cut the conversation off and tell him to contact my brother-in-law because he oversaw the finances. This wasn't untrue, but it was mostly my sister who handled the finances, as part of our initial divide-and-conquer plan for how to care for our dad.

The truth is we did have to pay for part of my dad's care; the VA and Social Security covered almost half of it, and we split the remainder three ways. When he moved to skilled nursing and memory care, the monthly amount for his care doubled, if not tripled, and we had to find a way to finance it. We were able to find a state program in Washington to help, but it required a great deal of time, phone calls, and more. The place where he lived did not want the hassle of dealing with any funding source; therefore, all the money came into the joint checking account, and my sister paid for the facility directly.

It is imperative that if you are outsourcing care or have your loved one in a care facility, you understand their financing requirements up front. Some facilities will require you to sign over assets for your loved one. Knowing this could be the case is one reason we liquidated my dad's assets before finalizing a new place for him to live.

One important lesson we learned the hard way is that shared checking accounts are not always the right thing to do depending on the state you live in for many reasons, such as fraud or claims of fraud. In our case, we had all my dad's money transferred into a joint checking account administered by my sister and me. And when my dad passed away, despite us being on this account, we had not completed the paperwork for the funds to be payable upon death. Therefore, when the bank received notification of my dad's death, the checking account was frozen even though we were listed on the account. It took several weeks to access the funds, but we finally did.

Shabnam

On one of my trips home to Malaysia, when my parents were still doing okay but obviously aging—Mum was almost eighty and Dad was eighty-six—I decided to go through all their files and organize things, as I knew they had lost the energy and drive that they'd previously had. Mum had done all the house management and paying of bills, while Dad had done the international wires for sending money to educate us and take care of family members in India and Pakistan. But neither of them was particularly good at keeping track of assets and the formal paperwork.

As I went through several file drawers' worth of papers, I found that Dad had been buying stocks of Indian companies throughout his career. There were dozens of stock certificates! And while browsing through the papers, I recognized names like Tata and Birla, companies that had become super successful, so those stocks were probably worth a lot. My brother and I started to write to the companies to see how we could convert the stocks into cash.

It turned out that my father's signature had changed from his Parkinson's, and it no longer matched his signature from his healthy younger days. The Indian companies and lawyers wanted him to travel in person to India to verify his identity—but his Parkinson's had worsened and he could not make the trip. At the time of this writing, it is seven years past his end and we are still trying to get the legal clearance in India to access those shares.

We feel so sad that his hard work over so many decades may all be wasted because we didn't anticipate this and didn't pay attention to where his assets were located and how they would be able to come to the family down the road. This is a key takeaway: Track the money! Make an inventory of the assets in place, make sure the paperwork and signatures are current, and have a plan for how to deal with the assets when the owner is no longer able. We also should have signed on as co-owners to bank accounts and property; a few simple things up front would have made a world of difference.

My parents ran out of money in the last ten years of their lives—or so they thought. Actually, they had a lot. It just wasn't in a place and form that they could access. So please take an inventory and have clarity. My parents lived very simply on an academic salary all their lives and yet the small amounts of investments they'd made had grown. Unfortunately, the money was inaccessible to them when they needed it, and the value of the stocks may be lost to us completely.

CHAPTER TAKEAWAYS

It is important to recognize that when you are a caregiver, compassion is not enough. You need to prepare both legally and financially. A critical first step is to get a reputable elder law attorney in the state where your loved one resides and have them help you clarify the documentation you need. The legal part of this journey includes wills, POA, durable POA, and living wills—legally binding documents that are all critical to being able to manage caregiving and the processes after death. Understanding insurance coverage, financial structures, assets, liabilities, and accounts is part of this journey, and having these documents in place is a real stress reducer, which you are going to need. If you take anything away from this chapter, start with expert advice, prioritize documentation, review insurance and finances, and seek help from someone who can help you keep organized.

3

The Place of Care

One of the most fundamental questions in caregiving has to do with *where* that care will take place. This single decision has huge implications for everything else that will occur around it, and therefore it should be made thoughtfully and, preferably, early and with acknowledgment of how emotional the decision will be for the seniors. Giving up one's home and independence is such a psychologically fraught idea that we try to avoid it as an option until it is often too late. But the reality is that at some point in the life journey there will likely be a situation where one parent or both elders cannot manage to live in their home—or require an intense level of in-home care that is expensive and hard to put in place without heavy supervision and oversight.

Why is this so hard to solve? Home is a combination of safety, security, comfort, and personal memories. It is also a declaration of independence and freedom. And the alternatives—assisted living, nursing home facilities, long-term care, hospitals—all signal to us levels of increasing lack of control and personal space and decreasing quality of life. As our population ages, however, the reality of having to move from one's home to an alternative living arrangement with more support and less independence is becoming more and more common and necessary. The nuclear family model that is common now means that fewer seniors have enough younger adult family members available to enable them to live at home.

As our population ages and this need for a variety of assisted living arrangements becomes imperative, there are companies racing to provide options. Options such as redesigning homes to allow for wheelchairs and limited mobility, platforms for identifying temporary and in-home carers, long-term care insurance to cover costs, and more are increasing but are nowhere near adequate for the demand. Waitlists for better nursing homes can be ten to fifteen years and cost up to $20,000 per month! This problem is not theoretical; we are living it already today.

For caregivers and elders, it is essential to take a pragmatic approach to planning various scenarios. Leaving the decision to when there is a crisis is the worst-case scenario because there is a long lead time in finding options and getting access. We need to all be thinking about when, how, and where will we live for each stage of health and functionality ahead—not just if and when we need help.

Ideally, we should work up a rough plan for what is ahead and start making those options available. Most importantly, we need to have the conversation and be realistic and come to an agreement with the key stakeholders involved. This includes determining who is responsible for what and how decision-making will happen when choices need to be adjusted. Having the conversation and documenting it can make a world of difference later on. We need planning for the journey that comes before the end of life, with a goal of making it wholistic and practical with the greatest quality of life for everyone who is involved. Here is what we'll cover in this chapter:

- Types of living arrangements
- Finding the right place to live for your specific situation
- Potential transitions in care settings

TYPES OF LIVING ARRANGEMENTS

Outside the legal and financial considerations, one of the next areas to discuss is where your loved one will live. There are many options to consider including:

- *Aging in place:* Loved ones stay in their home with or without caregivers; an option growing in popularity for independent seniors and elders.
- *House sharing:* Seniors who can live independently share a home to reduce costs.
- *Moving in with family:* If there is space and time, some families prefer to move their loved ones

into their own homes. This can be cost-effective, though it may require some home modifications. This is sometimes an intermediary step to other kinds of assisted living.

* *Independent living communities:* Homes, townhomes, or apartments typically for those who don't need assistance with their daily activities. Often, these are specifically senior apartment communities, only taking tenants over a certain age.

* *Assisted living facilities:* Sometimes called nursing homes or continuing care retirement communities; can include long-term care that varies but typically offers a variety of service levels to those who may need some help with activities of daily living. And often they can elevate care if needed.

* *Respite care:* Short-term care in an assisted living or skilled nursing community that is intended to give primary caregivers a rest.

* *Memory care units:* Specialized parts of assisted living that specifically support people with Alzheimer's or other forms of dementia.

* *Skilled nursing facilities:* Offer specialized medical care provided by licensed professionals and are for patients who need short-term rehabilitation or medical treatments after hospital stays. Not the same as long-term care facilities. If you are using insurance, there is typically a set number of days allowed in a skilled nursing facility.

Shari

The main issue about my dad's caregiving place was that he wanted to stay in South Dakota, which he considered home. But he had no help there, because my sister and I lived in Washington State with our families and my brother was in Minnesota. We struggled to have clear conversations with my dad about this, as he was already experiencing dementia.

Because of his condition, he was not fully able to know or admit to his impending demise. I believe my dad had a fear of dying, but his greatest fears were dying alone in a hospital or nursing home, being unable to take care of himself, and being a burden on his family. Knowing these goals was very helpful for us as we moved through the last stages of life with my dad.

A key turning point, aside from the driver's license, was our decision to sell the house my dad lived in. My husband and I owned it, having bought it from my dad when we lived in Italy. We needed a tax shelter, but we also knew the house was a powerful tie to South Dakota. The sooner we could sever that tie, the easier the transition would be for everyone. Selling the house meant he needed a place to live.

We tag-teamed the difficult task of telling Dad that we were selling the house and that moving in with one of us was the most logical option. Still, I had to accept that the outcome I was hoping for—the one where my dad would leap up and say, *Thank you, my brilliant daughter, I can't wait to move out of the state I've lived in for eighty-two years!*—was never going to happen.

To complicate things, my dad had a roommate: his former wife. After my mother passed away, my dad remarried. South

Dakota is a common property state, and the law requires spouses to be responsible for each other's healthcare costs and estate. My dad and his then wife had quietly dissolved their marriage—a painful decision for a devoted Catholic like him, even if the church had come to accept divorce. Despite the legal split, his former wife continued living in the house. She had the primary bedroom; my dad slept on the den floor for years until I visited and discovered the arrangement. To move things forward, we coordinated with her family. My brother let them know we were intending to sell the house and move my dad out of state. They were understanding and soon found her a new place to live, removing one more worry.

We received and accepted an offer on the house. After months of dancing around the issue, I had to have the conversation: "Dad, we sold the house. You're moving to Washington to be closer to us."

While my dad did not get angry, he pushed back and dug in his heels. But we really gave him no options. What helped him make the final decision was that he did not have a place to live in South Dakota, he did not have a car, and all his grandchildren were on the West Coast. I emphasized how much his family—especially his grandchildren—needed him. I didn't offer an out, but I did say he could always visit South Dakota. Although he accepted the decision, I could tell he was holding on to the hope that he'd return someday, and to me this sounded acceptable.

My brother took charge of moving my dad out to Washington, while I looked for the right place for him to land. It was quite a journey, literally and figuratively. To make the most of the move, my brother scheduled a cross-country trip, driving our dad and a favorite uncle to Dad's new home. They took back roads and stopped to see family, turning it into a beautiful adventure for two old friends who had spent every holiday together for decades.

While I summarized this move to look like a quick and easy process, it was not. It was years in the making. I could never have anticipated how stressful it would be, and there are many reasons for that. When my dad was very early in his dementia, he was not making good decisions, so we had to start doing that for him. While stepping into this role was hard enough, I wasn't able at that time to process the grief caused by the rapid transition. As I reflect on it, I ingested massive amounts of grief, shame, and loss that I buried deep inside, only for them to emerge years later.

Unprocessed grief for your body is like what kryptonite is for Superman. It will find you whether or not you try to bury it. It will all eventually come out. I tried working, exercising, and running away from it, but it did not leave. What I do know is that grief is not exclusive; it consumes everything. It turns the world you know just a little gray. And while I understood intellectually that what we were doing was the right thing, emotionally I did not want to do anything to hurt my dad.

FINDING THE RIGHT PLACE TO LIVE

If aging in place, house sharing, or living with family and friends are the chosen options, it is best to start looking at what is needed now and what might be needed in the future to accommodate caregiving. This includes possible mobility issues, such as stairs, location of the restroom, type of bathing options, and meal requirements or options. For example, if the elder cannot cook, they will need to have care to support food shopping, preparation, and feeding. When caregiving at home, many have transformed living spaces into rooms for loved ones. If palliative or hospice care is involved, these services will often help source the proper types of beds and furniture. This is often the preface for loved ones to die at home, a wish for many. Constant caregiving can be stressful for family, so remember that home health services like Senior Helpers or Visiting Angels are great resources for support.

House sharing has become a more popular option, where, in some cases, two to five individuals live in a more intimate setting with a range of care options. This is a good choice if your loved one is not particularly social or needs more full-time care. In addition, there is also respite care, depending on the condition of the person you are caregiving for, which you can find by searching in your local area.

The other option is to look for a facility where your loved one can live, and this depends on the condition of the individual, type of care needed, and budget. These facilities range from very basic to extremely luxurious, with prices to match. Depending on many factors, insurance may not cover the cost, so be aware of terms before signing up. Independent and assisted living communities also have a unique feel and can offer a very social setting with many activities and progressive care. They often have levels of care so you can start in a senior apartment and, as care needs change, progress to the more elevated care needs area. In some cases, they have memory care or skilled nursing facilities within them to make it easier to elevate care as needed. Memory care units are usually locked facilities for the safety of residents.

Shabnam

Living arrangements for my parents had to be considered twice, once when they were both together and then again when it was just my mother alone. With my parents in Malaysia and all three children in different countries, the decision was pretty major. My parents used to travel to the US when they were healthy, but at some point my father's Parkinson's made that impossible; the flight alone was twenty hours and too strenuous for him.

We had talked about them moving to the US permanently, but they were reluctant to give up their friends and community, Dad's work, and all the comforts they could afford with labor being cheaper in Malaysia (a full-time live-in helper cost about $200 per month). Healthcare in Malaysia was a fifth of the cost in the US, with excellent doctors, so there was no compromise in the quality of medical care they could access. They had a physical therapist come to the house two or three times a week, and hospital care was excellent and close by. So when things were fairly stable, the decision to stay in Malaysia made total sense.

However, when crises happened, like my father breaking his leg or getting severe pneumonia, there was no one on-site to manage decisions. This is when it was hardest being a primary caregiver halfway across the world (and other than the extreme time difference, the situation is the same if you are in a different city or state). That is when I questioned our choice to have them live far away. It was extremely stressful for them and for me and my siblings, and by the time we realized that, it was too late to move them. I also could not have replicated their daily living support without an enormous expense in the US.

When my father was in the hospital having surgery for his broken leg, it took me a few days to get over to Malaysia, and those in-between days were so difficult, as I could not track what was happening in the hospital. My brother Pervez had flown over from Melbourne, so fortunately he took charge. I had my alarm set to ring every two hours through the nights so I could talk to the surgeon, anesthesiologist, neurologist, nurses, and so on. And then I would go to work, having not slept much at all. I remember thinking, *This is like having a newborn baby to take care of all night long, except I don't get the joy of a lovely new baby and feeling thrilled.* My children, having seen what I went through with parents halfway across the world, say, "Please do not do to us what you had to go through; please live close by or at least on the same continent."

Once my father passed away, and Mum was formally diagnosed with dementia, we had another choice to make. Bring her to the US so I could have peace of mind and check in on her frequently, or leave her in Malaysia without a family member? I spoke to her neurologist who said that the move would be impossible for my mother. In a state of dementia, she would not be able to take the shock of a whole new environment; it would most likely lead to a rapid decline. So the choice was really not a choice at all, and once again we had to think about the best way to give her a comfortable, safe, and relatively good life without children or family nearby.

My goal had been to have both parents live out their final years in their home. It was a lovely, comfortable apartment and had all the conveniences nearby so their helpers could easily make the household function. Pharmacies, groceries, and the dentist all were within walking distance. So it was a sensible place for my mother to live, except that her children could not visit often. I went every four months or so, and my brothers went over a few times a year. We all hope we can have as comfortable a life as hers was when we are in the final stage.

However, when the Covid pandemic struck, it was a nightmare. The Malaysian border was closed to foreigners for almost two years. We could not go to our mother, and she was so incredibly sad and could not understand why no one was visiting. I was heartbroken when Mum would say, "Don't say you will come to visit because I know you won't." How could I explain a pandemic and closed borders to someone who was now like a child? That time period was one none of us could have imagined, but it has shaped my own view for the future. That situation could happen again, and being on the same landmass as family seems important in a different way now.

So when making choices on where to locate your parents, there are things you can anticipate and control, and there is all the rest. No amount of money is useful if you don't have a plan. One way to improve decision-making is to acknowledge the fact that there will be an end-of-life phase. It could be sudden and short, such as when a loved one has a heart attack or late-stage cancer, or it could be longer, such as with strokes or Parkinson's. Regardless, there is a final stage and it is worth thinking and planning a bit around that, especially with siblings and spouses. Is there someone who can or will take the lead? Does it make sense for the parent(s) to move before there is a crisis? What is the trade-off to losing their friends and comfort zone? And when would be a good time for a move?

What if there are no children? I have a dear friend, Dan, who has no children and lost his wife. He went into a deep depression and was found unconscious on the floor when neighbors called the police for a wellness check. Dan's closest family member is a niece in Dallas, and as the only primary caregiver left, she had to make decisions going forward. I also recently met a couple, Steve and Ann, who decided to sell their Florida house and move into an assisted care facility in North Carolina because they have no children and wanted to make sensible decisions for themselves. They are caregivers for themselves and had to make tough but practical decisions, which is admirable.

I am having these discussions with my two children in a more open way, because my experience with my parents obviously makes me ponder what will happen for me and my husband and how I want to plan around that. It feels empowering, not morbid. We should all get more comfortable talking about death and how we want to shape our end-of-life stage as best possible. This doesn't mean it's all easy, though. When things have not yet become impossible to manage, it is very difficult to make drastic changes, even if they may be necessary for the long run. Also, managing the practical reality of adding on new responsibilities across adult children who are facing full and stressful lives of their own is challenging. These are all heavy but necessary conversations to have together.

POTENTIAL TRANSITIONS IN CARE SETTINGS

Skilled nursing and advanced care are often difficult to find or have long waiting lists, so it's essential to understand the options and their costs. What is the future of your caregiving? When you are caring for those who are aging or have terminal conditions, you need to understand that these conditions are not going to reverse but will instead progress. With this mindset, you can plan accordingly and look for places that offer options for transitions in care.

As needs elevate and the end of life approaches, there are facilities that specialize in this type of care, and the focus and precision with which they deliver can be very beneficial. For example, hospice—whether at home or in a hospital or hospice-specific facility—is focused on comfort care only, no lifesaving measures. This level of focus is what many people need to know that their loved ones are cared for properly. So keep this in mind when planning the future of caregiving.

Shari

When my dad made it to Washington, the next step was looking for the right place to live. Unfortunately, my dad did not want to live with us. While he was growing up, his Irish grandmother lived with his family. I don't know much about her other than she only wore black, grieving her husband who had died many years prior. It was apparently not the best situation, because he swore he'd never do that to his own children. My dad wanted nothing to do with the decision, so we handled the search for a retirement community. And per usual, he put the decision on me.

We went on tours of our top choices. If I had the kids with me, I would try to make it fun. For them, the idea of having Papa Joe live close to us was all they needed to hear; they were so excited. After touring several options and then narrowing it down to two retirement communities, each offered to have my dad do trial stays to determine which one he liked better.

Brilliant idea, I thought. My dad was social, so I figured I'd drop him off, he'd find someone to talk to, and when I picked him up, he would thank me and say, *This is the one. I met so many great people, thank you.* Yes, very naive of me, but everyone can dream. While my dad was willing to do the trial stays, he did not socialize much. We picked one together and got him set up, though it was painful to leave him there. I, along with my siblings, felt strongly about honoring our dad's wishes.

The place we selected was very close to our house, and we eventually moved into another home even closer. We selected the place primarily for its social aspect and strong community. Each time we visited, residents could be seen in common areas, on the front patio, walking outside, or boarding the bus for community outings. This was what my dad needed, and it gave us the opportunity to see him daily and even have the kids hang out with him in his cool apartment.

The first few months were rough. My dad was sad, did not want to engage with people, and really just wanted to go home. I felt like I had done this to him and likened it to the experience of dropping a child off at school. I was visiting multiple times a day to make sure he was okay, sign him up for events, and get him out to do things. It was very hard. Slowly, things began to normalize as he started meeting people, sharing his story, and listening to others. It was working. The GI Generation is such a beautiful one: They just enjoy community, and once this clicked into gear, everything got better. The dementia did kick in at times, and he would let me know he just wanted to go home, but we would try to refocus him on gratitude for being close to his family. My dad went most places with us—swim meets, soccer games, basketball, school activities. It was really special for our kids and for me.

I did feel like we had the best of both worlds. While he wasn't in the house with us, he was a five-minute drive or a fifteen-minute run away. In the summer, the kids would ride their bikes down to see him and have lunch or just hang out, and my dad still had everything he wanted. His apartment was comfortable, the community delivered the right amount of social engagement, and he also spent a great deal of time on outings. Everything was moving along well and then Covid hit. Trying to explain to my dad why we weren't visiting, why he could not leave, why we would stand outside with masks on and talk on the phone or through the window was very hard. But I was grateful he was in that community, and they did their best to follow the rules and keep the residents safe and comfortable.

The cost was something that we struggled with, and I know these communities are becoming more and more expensive. If you can have the conversation with your loved one about their wishes, be up front and realistic with them about the reality of the cost. This will help you get to a place that works for everyone.

If it had been his decision alone, my dad probably would

have opted to stay in South Dakota, but after many years of having this conversation with him, he did tell me that he felt better being closer to his grandchildren. And the truth is, we wouldn't have seen much of him if he had stayed in South Dakota. Also, when you have a loved one with dementia, it is really hard to have them be unattended many states away. They need family, care, and sometimes privacy to age without the judgment of others. We wanted my dad to have the ability to age and progress in his dementia with grace and dignity.

CHAPTER TAKEAWAYS

Safety and security are always top of mind when caregiving. And while the question of where a loved one is going to live is not an easy decision for a number of reasons, it is necessary. Be informed about the potential future needs of your loved one, the types of facilities available in the area where you're loved one will be living, and what the waiting times and costs are like. Be prepared for this to be a very emotionally charged topic. Moving someone out of their home or modifying their home to be safer is a difficult conversation.

INTERLUDE

Accepting Uncertainty

Shari

One key part of caregiving is being able to accept uncertainty. As my dad's dementia progressed, we did not know what to expect when we showed up to see him daily. He was always a sharp dresser, and his typical outfit was pants—or slacks, as he called them—an undershirt, a button-down shirt or polo, a cardigan sweater, and wing tips or dress shoes. He never wore jeans, sweatpants, sneakers, or T-shirts—and I mean never. Even after walking up and down the aisles of the hardware store he owned with my mother for years, he never left home without his leather-soled wing tips.

As he started to decline, we started to notice things change. One day, I showed up and he had on his tank undershirt and two cardigans. He was legally blind, so understandably he could not see he wasn't wearing a shirt. He felt the buttons and went on. He also started to mix up his days and nights. In the Pacific Northwest, we have absolutely the best summer nights; at the peak of summer, it will stay light until after 10:00 p.m. I think it is Mother Nature's way of making up for November through January. This confused my dad, who had never experienced that before. So after dinner, if he fell asleep and woke up at 8:00 p.m., he would often think it was the next morning and start his routine only to find the breakfast room empty and the place quiet. I did my best to make him feel like it was not a big deal and that this happened to everyone.

After he moved into memory care, this uncertainty accelerated. When he was hospitalized for a fall, they put him on hefty antipsychotic drugs. Because of Covid protocols, we could not stay with him in the hospital, and he was confused and scared when he woke up. After the first night, he was barely coherent when I visited with him the next day. He had not slept well and was very agitated. The medical team heavily medicated him and put restraints on him. It was awful, but I understood the reasoning. This persisted throughout the week, and he was different each time I arrived. He needed help going to the bathroom and was very uncomfortable with the female nurses and aides helping him.

When we got him into memory care, his disposition was about the same and he was in a different state every day when we arrived. We had them stop giving him antipsychotics and when they wore off, some of his cognitive functions came back, but they were not consistent. He could use his legs and walker one day, but other days he could not and needed a wheelchair. You learn to adapt and be prepared for anything. The biggest risk was falling. He was so used to his freedom that he did not fully understand his limitations. He had bruises, which made me very concerned, so I started showing up more randomly to check on him and verify his care. It turned out that, often, he would get up in the middle of the night to use the restroom and fall. It got so bad they started putting his mattress on the floor to prevent him from hurting himself.

At the time, he was in hospice care, which was helpful because they were there to make sure he was safe. Then, the unexpected happened. The hospice nurse called to tell me that because my dad was gaining weight, they were going to drop him from hospice care. I had no idea what this meant for his health long term, but I did know that when we'd accepted hospice care, we'd had to remove him from his VA benefits. Getting someone back into VA health care is not easy once you've dropped it.

This moved us from a land of uncertainty to a universe of complete stress. So, for more than a month, I was my dad's primary physician and caregiver. My sister, who was out of state, took on trying to find a more permanent solution. The memory care facility from where he'd been released had a doctor who would check in on patients occasionally, and we met with him a couple of times for advice. Still, because my dad was not technically under his care, he was unable to help much.

I was still juggling my job on top of the full-time caregiving, and at one point I had to go on a business trip. My brother came to take over, and there was an incident where my dad's arm started to swell up to double its size. My brother checked with the memory care staff, but they were unfortunately not able to help much. The one thing my brother did notice was the rings on my dad's fingers needed to come off because of the swelling. My brother is a former firefighter who built fire trucks for a living. He called the local firehouse on a non-emergency call, and they came over to cut the rings off my dad's fingers. After a few days, my dad's arm returned to normal.

Then, when I returned, it happened again. This time, I was able to get the memory care doctor to take a look. He determined it was a circulation problem and offered to call a transport company to take my dad to the hospital. I didn't want to put my father through the stress and confusion of sitting in a hospital waiting room; the last time we'd been there, we'd waited sixteen hours. I was also anxious because I had to attend an event that evening. I felt guilty for leaving, but I also had no idea what the right answer was. It was a very stressful time. My dad's arm went back down to normal size, but his care remained challenging. I was caregiving for him, taking care of my children and our household, working, and making stressful medical decisions with my siblings.

I was finally able to convince hospice to come and reevaluate my father. His condition was declining, and one Saturday he started taking very short and shallow breaths. I had a priest come over and give him last rites because I did not know what to expect. My dad had been a devout Catholic his whole life and was adamant early on that he wanted last rites to be performed before his death. On that day, my dad was very confused and having a hard time speaking. He was in and out of lucidity often and thought I was his mom or sister. When the priest began, he asked my dad to recite prayers with him. All of a sudden, it was as if he had become another person. My dad recited the blessings and prayers he had been saying all his life without missing a word. It was incredible.

After we completed the last rites, I told the priest I couldn't believe that he had been able to say all the prayers because he'd been primarily incoherent all day. The priest stopped, smiled, and said, "Yes, it is beautiful. Prayers are often buried deep within us and can come out when needed, but you never really forget them."

I still get tears in my eyes when I think of this moment. No matter what your religious or spiritual beliefs about what happens after we die, there is a beauty in the certainty of faith. My dad held on to that certainty despite his dementia. It also showed me a bigger picture outside the uncertainty I had been experiencing through the caregiving journey. No matter what you believe, it is a comfort to know how deep some memories and beliefs are buried within us.

PART TWO

The Caregiving Life

4

Assembling and Managing Care

One thing that is a guarantee with caregiving is that you cannot do it alone. Even if you are a primary caregiver, you will be reliant on many different types of people as you go through the journey. Some of your care team will be close family members who share responsibility, and some may be close friends or neighbors who voluntarily help; others may be professionals, such as healthcare providers and paid help, while others may be from communities that form through a shared interest, such as religion or disease-specific support.

Each group has its own set of obligations and motivations, its own set of rules and structures by which it operates, and that all determines how care is given. It is useful to think about all the different types of people and communities you can (or need to) work with so that you can most effectively deliver the best possible care for your loved one.

The people and communities that end up being a resource to you in your caregiving journey are sometimes obvious and sometimes completely unexpected, but in all cases their contributions are deeply meaningful and should be appreciated. This chapter provides ideas and advice on strategies for working with, and even developing beforehand, the support that you will need at some point. Building good relationships with those who are likely to be in your care team circles (siblings, partners, children, healthcare providers, friends and neighbors, and so on) will be something to be grateful for when caregiving presents you with challenges, so invest in those relationships early and broadly.

This chapter discusses the following:

- The basics of creating a care team
- Options for outsourcing care
- The hybrid model of care
- Caring for the whole person

CREATING A CARE TEAM

Setting up a care plan and team means that when care is needed, you can execute the plan without taking on all the burden yourself. What this requires is understanding the caregiving needs of your loved one and building a plan around them. A great place to start is creating a daily schedule and establishing roles for those who need to be involved.

For example, if you are sharing caretaking, have a home health aide, or have a loved one in assisted living, one person will need to be the main point of contact for the assisted living facility. If you have to travel, especially for your job, you may need to work through who will take care of daily activities when you aren't available—siblings, friends, or paid caregivers? To begin, assess your resources and determine who can be part of your care team.

Siblings

If you have siblings, they are usually the first line of defense for your loved one's care team. We know that families can be complicated, and modern life often has families living in separate locations, which can make assembling a caregiving team more complicated.

But wherever they are, siblings are likely going to work together in some way to jointly care for their parents. This gets interesting because every sibling has their own expectations, limitations, skills, personality, and life. There are stories across the spectrum—siblings working well together, siblings who were missing in action, siblings who took turns to pull out all the stops, siblings who fought over every decision. Even though siblings are partners by default and not necessarily by choice, there are reasons to make the best of a joint caregiving journey and establish strategies for working together effectively.

In an ideal scenario, your siblings are your closest allies, and you can all pull together to care for your parents, perhaps even building stronger connections in the process. As with other members of your care team, principles of respect, kindness, and open communication go a long way toward getting through a caregiving phase together. Lean on your siblings when you can and find ways that everyone can contribute, even though it may be in different ways and at different times. A good rule of thumb is that this process is not about having equal tasks; it is about leveraging the unique skills and resources across your sibling care team.

Here are some suggestions on working with your siblings:

- Don't assume anything, ask a lot of questions early on, and be open to listening even if you disagree. Some questions to consider:
  - How do we each feel about managing our parents' end-of-life care?
  - What are our goals?
  - What are our fears?
  - Are we clear about what our parents would like?
- Establish some general principles on how to share the care:
  - What are the skills each of us brings?
  - What time commitment do we each have?
  - Who will be the primary caregiver, and how will others share and support?
- Discuss and document everything. Have an open communication approach and record what was decided for reference. You should write down and share:
  - What you agreed on.
  - What needs to be done going forward (and who is in charge of what).
  - Information about budgets: how much is

available in your parents' assets, how much you anticipate will be needed, who will cover the gap if any.

- What choices are available and how you will make decisions.
- What happens if you disagree.
- Schedule periodic check-ins to make sure you are in sync with what is happening and aligned on the situation. This might be daily when there is a crisis or monthly when care is stable.
- Effective icebreakers can make a big difference in drawing out the underlying thoughts of each sibling and leave everyone more aware and tuned in to the factors that will inform care. For example, use the Rose/Bud/Thorn approach (a method developed by the Boy Scouts of America) for dialogue on any topic:
  - Rose: What is one thing you appreciate or celebrate?
  - Bud: What is something in the works that could become a positive soon?
  - Thorn: What is one thing that is a concern?
- Be willing to adapt as needed. Things change in all our lives, so the care model has to change with it.
- Be kind and respectful. We are all stressed and busy, and caregiving can take more energy and time and money than anyone ever imagined. Give grace and kindness to your siblings and ask for it yourself.

Shabnam

My elder brother, Pervez, was always the first one on the scene when there was a crisis with our father. He lived in Australia, so that meant a seven-hour flight to Malaysia versus my twenty-one-hour flight from New Jersey. Our other brother, Ariff, lived in San Francisco and would fly out when he could, but he had less flexibility.

One time, when my father's lungs, weakened by Parkinson's, caused pneumonia severe enough to require hospitalization, I spent several days living out of the hospital room with my father. I was beyond stressed and exhausted, and then Ariff showed up; he had just flown in from California. It was such a relief to see him! While it was not the best of circumstances, given our dad was in pain and struggling, it meant everything to be able to share the burden with my sibling.

Ariff had come straight from the airport after flying halfway around the world. Right away he sent me home to take a shower and get some sleep, and he stayed the whole night in the hospital with just a mat on the floor. I came back refreshed the next morning, alight with the realization of what a blessing it was to have a brother willing to step in. He cared so sweetly for my father, and it still warms my heart to this day.

During that and other difficult periods, I felt thankful for my siblings and not having to manage everything myself. Just knowing that backup resources were available to share the physical and emotional burdens of parent care helped immensely. In a best-case scenario, siblings work seamlessly together to share caregiving responsibilities—but best-case isn't a given. Mostly, we muddle through the dividing up of care, and maybe the best-case scenario is that siblings come out of parent care without having feelings of resentment, anger, and frustration.

While my brothers did show up when it was most necessary, I did most of the practical things associated with my parents' care over the last ten years of their lives. My brothers must have known I was managing all this, but I wonder if they (or anyone) really knew how much work and time and energy and thinking went into keeping all the balls in the air. There were definitely moments I could have used more help from my brothers, but somehow it rarely occurred to me to ask for more hands-on help.

Somehow, things kept going and we all carried on, but now, looking back, I realize my situation is probably very similar to what many people experience. One person (often, but not always, a daughter) takes on the bulk of the tasks—and rebalancing never quite happens. This can lead to frustration on the part of the primary caregiver. It is a point we can do better addressing and handling all through the caregiving journey because all siblings have an equal responsibility, and even though each sibling will have constraints, it is likely that all can do better working together more fairly and jointly. Playing to the strengths of each one while also highlighting the full scope of work required and being more objective about the overall workload would be a great way for siblings to handle caregiving.

Take the example of Kathy, who is currently the primary caregiver for both her parents. She has a brother and a sister who each have the potential to do a lot more, but somehow Kathy became the majority caregiver. Despite asking repeatedly, she cannot get her siblings to step up and contribute more. When they do step in to help, they make her feel like they are doing her a favor rather than just selflessly helping out. Rather than compromise her parents' care, she continues to do the heavy lifting.

There are also incredibly positive examples of siblings working together. Claudia has a mother in her eighties who requires heavy care and recently had surgery. Claudia's father passed away recently after also requiring significant care. Claudia and her brother have tag-teamed throughout all this and provided loving, practical care; even their kids help out regularly. While her brother lives close to their parent and is the primary caregiver, Claudia brought their mother to live with her for two years when her brother needed a break.

Another friend is one of seven children, and when their father had a stroke, each child came for a week to be the caregiver. They each said it was among the best times they'd ever had with their father and served to create lasting, positive memories.

Another example of positive shared sibling care is Angela's story. When her mother was diagnosed with cancer, Angela moved her in and took care of her for two years through cancer therapy. She eventually burned out and had to quit her job. Staying at home with her mother actually proved even harder than juggling her job and caregiving! Angela appealed to her sister, who then moved their mother in with her. Angela went back to work—it gave her a welcome change and was therapeutic, as she could work without the stress of being a primary caregiver.

Looking back, I wish I'd had more regular tactical discussions with my brothers. If we could have had periodic reviews of how things were going, what our goals were, what changes needed to be made, and how we individually and together were handling caregiving, things could have been better. Even just talking and listening, making space to be heard and understood, is so important to avoid feeling resentful and angry. It seems so obvious, but we don't do it! If we approach caregiving like a team project at work, I think we would do much better achieving positive outcomes for both parents and caregivers.

Partners

Spouses and partners are an integral part of the caregiving journey. Transparency is critical to reducing stress, and the more you can share the better. Also, anyone who is out of the loop can feel disenfranchised. Spouses and partners, whether they are helping with caregiving or offering support by taking over tasks like childcare or household needs, are crucial for this journey.

In addition, it is very easy to disassociate when you become overwhelmed, but partners will notice changes in your emotional state and can be a safe space for you. They may not be able to solve all your problems, but sometimes just having a listener to make sure you don't forget yourself is important.

When caregiving, time is very thin, and partners in particular can find themselves very low on the list of priorities. And as caregiving intensifies, so can the distance between you and your partner. It is best to acknowledge this potential struggle early on and find ways to bridge the gap so it does not widen.

Shari

I first met my husband walking through the halls of my high school. In our small town everyone knew everyone, and even if you weren't hanging out together, you at least knew each other. My husband was a new kid: tall, blond, blue-eyed, and built like a typical farm boy. He had kind eyes and a quiet, shy demeanor, as many do when they are new to school. We ended up sitting across from each other in history class—and the rest is history! We married fourteen years later and started our family.

He has always been my champion and my rock. The kind of person that makes me feel like I can do anything. We were already married with two growing kids when I started to get very concerned about my dad and his well-being. My husband was supportive and tried to reach me when I went deep into my world of disassociation as things were becoming too overwhelming. I heard him when he said, "You need to take a break" or "You are going too hard," but I didn't really listen. I didn't stop. I truly don't think I knew how. All I knew was one direction, forward and fast. If I got stuck, I would pause for a moment and rock the car back and forth until I became unstuck, so I could push forward again, right back on the same road.

My husband's role on the care team was to help at home and keep me from slipping too far into disassociation. After my father passed away, he said in his serious voice, "You have to take a break. I am worried about you."

"Worried, why?" I asked. If I am honest, I knew why: I existed at that time, but I was not living. Between caregiving, our children, and work, I had totally lost connection with myself. I was just going through the motions to keep the train on the tracks. And when that happens, you lose connection with your loved ones as well. You can't be connected to others if you have no connection to yourself. It just isn't possible.

While I feel very fortunate to be one of the lucky ones with a supportive spouse, I would be lying if I said caregiving didn't affect our relationship. I became a former champion at disassociation; I gave it up after years and decided that I'd rearrange my life around being present. He had spent some time trying to help me realize that, but I did not want to see or admit that he was right. I needed to slow down. I wish I had entered therapy earlier so someone could have helped me see what my husband was trying to tell me. My avoidance stemmed from a long history of caregiving, trauma from my mother's illness, poor boundaries, and profound grief. You can tell by my ability to name these things that I am doing the work to get through it.

As a partner, you can support a caregiving spouse by strengthening communication, calling things the way you see them, and understanding if they can't address issues in the moment. Oftentimes, resentment lives in silence, and having a free space to speak openly is a necessity. Another helpful thing is to not try too hard to find a solution or fix something unless asked. Sometimes an ear is the best gift you can give.

If you are caregiving or the partner of a caregiver, learn how to set boundaries; know your limits and be clear about them. Share some of the caregiving load and encourage breaks and time together. Know the signs for when your loved one is pushing the limits, and get them to seek some help.

The Extended Circle—Friends, Neighbors, Colleagues, Others

The caregiving team extends often beyond just your family. It typically flows into friends, neighbors, colleagues, and others who may be able to offer some kind of support. This holds true whether your loved one is at home or in a facility. The biggest milestone to be reached here is the ability to ask for help when needed. These can be simple things, such as asking a neighbor to drop in to check on a loved one when you can't be around or checking up to see if a hired caregiver has any updates or needs. Sometimes it might simply be asking a friend to do school pickup if a loved one's appointment is running over. The care team is central to the journey, and the sooner it is built and in action, the more powerful your caregiving experience.

Shabnam

We all learned from the Covid pandemic that the separation between work and home is a fuzzy one, and life spills over both ways. Before the pandemic, we were less inclined to bring our full selves to the office, trying to keep a boundary between what was happening in our personal lives and what we were bringing to work. Now, there is more openness around how we integrate our work and home life. Being clear with your bosses and colleagues about your situation up front is key to managing your career and caregiving priorities.

There was a moment at work I remember clearly. I was in charge of a group of one hundred people, a patient support division in the US subsidiary of a Japanese pharmaceutical company. I got a call from my mother in Malaysia—she was hysterical because my father had fallen and broken his leg. They were waiting for the ambulance to show up, and he was in extreme pain. I was in budget season at work, on deadline for creating all kinds of financial projections about how resources should be allocated for the year ahead. It was a competitive process within the company, and one that stressed everyone out. And suddenly the reality hit—I was going to have to drop everything and fly to Malaysia to manage the crisis there.

I was so conflicted. I wanted to be responsible in my job and to my team (and of course, there is the struggle of feeling like no one else can do your job as well as you can). When I went, shell-shocked, to my boss, the response was "We have it covered, Shabnam. You go do what you need to do." Similar sentiments were repeated by both my US and Japanese colleagues, and I hope they know how much it meant to me. That moment of support and in the weeks ahead were so meaningful, an example to every manager and colleague in every company. I still count my blessings for the good and great people around me then.

All this takes so much trust. They trusted that I would be back to pick up when I could and continue to deliver for the company; I trusted that my team could do the work perfectly well without me. There was also such kindness and caring that the bonds between us as coworkers felt strengthened. In the three weeks that followed in Malaysia, I would check in on email, but not once was I asked, "When are you coming back?" There was no pressure, only support. To this day, I will do my utmost to support the company and my colleagues. This is what good working relationships and good company culture look like, and those are things to keep in mind when pondering career and job options.

A helping hand in caregiving can also come from unexpected members of your care team. When my father's Parkinson's was getting worse after a decent ten years, his neurologist recommended a physiotherapist come to the house two to three times a week. We met with the recommended physiotherapist, Dr. Arunkumar, and he began coming to the house to give my father exercises to do. Over the next few years, he became a close friend and direct caregiver for my parents. Dr. Arunkumar would assess their overall condition and write to me if anything seemed off.

When my father fell and broke his leg from not wanting to use his walking stick (oh, that fight for independence!), my mother called Dr. Arunkumar first, and he called the ambulance and showed up at the hospital. He was also, in a way, the default counselor for my father's mental well-being. Dr. Arunkumar would listen and be kind and present, a huge support in the absence of actual family members. My parents looked forward to his visits; it was as if all would be well as soon as he showed up, whether in calm moments or in crises.

In some ways, he took on much more responsibility than his official paid duties, and for me and my brothers, it was a huge relief that someone professional was checking in on our parents and available for a clear conversation as an adviser for care. So when you think of your caregiving team, think outside the box in terms of who can help more directly and support you in areas that you need. It may happen organically, as it did with Dr. Arunkumar, but it's also worth blue-skying for yourself: Is there a neighbor, a friend, or someone from your parents' community who can fill small or big gaps in your care management?

OUTSOURCING CARE

Sometimes, a professional is needed. Outsourcing care is a practical option to consider when caregiving. This typically means hiring agencies or services to handle some or all of the caregiving responsibilities. This applies to both home care and those living in facilities.

Benefits provided can range from medical care, companionship, personal care, household care, such as cleaning or meal prep, or physical or occupational services. These can help take some of the weight off the primary caregiver, but it is important to make sure that those brought into the home are reputable and that communication of expectations is very clear. Also, you need to understand the cost up front and whether insurance will pay for it. This can be a very helpful resource; just proceed with caution when you are selecting agencies and services, and make sure their workers have background checks and clear expectations. It is important to note that some of these agencies use aggressive and outdated marketing tactics, which can be reflective of the service they provide, so be cautious and selective when searching for the right service or agency.

Shabnam

Outsourcing care was a necessity since our family was spread across several continents. My parents lived in a comfortable condo and had a local caregiver, Pushpa, who took care of them on weekdays (and toward the end more often) for eighteen years. Pushpa became family over the years and continues to look after their place even though they are gone; to her, they were the parents she never had. Over time she became more than a helper and took on managing their day-to-day finances and doctors' appointments, triaging their needs, and keeping up communications with all the people they needed. It was a wonderful arrangement for us children because we trusted Pushpa like a family member and she was intrinsically kind and capable. As my parents' care needs increased, though, we realized they needed someone living with them.

So we did what many Asians do, we brought a caregiver from the Philippines to live with them. These were women who went to foreign countries seeking a way to earn income to support their families back home; they left their children and families and took two-year contracts. We had several women over the years, most of them good people, fortunately. At the end, we were especially lucky to have the most wonderful helper, Melissa. She was steady and intelligent and took charge of doctors' visits and managing my parents' needs in a quiet and strong way, never getting upset at my mother's increasingly erratic behavior from her dementia. We could not have asked for anyone better. Melissa and Pushpa learned to work well together and split up responsibilities according to their strengths and availability.

This was all the best part of outsourcing. But there were difficult and ugly parts too. One live-in helper ran away overnight with a boyfriend, taking a lot of diamond and gold jewelry. One of Dad's nurses later went to jail for beating a gentleman she was in charge of (it was caught on video). Imagine my guilt that I had placed her in charge of my dear loved ones who were vulnerable. Before Pushpa and Melissa, everything was ridiculously stressful. I had few backups, everything was based on word of mouth, and nothing was guaranteed or reliable or vetted. And nursing homes were a really, really bad option in Malaysia, so I was determined not to subject my darling parents to such an end. They deserved better.

In Asia, there is a taboo against putting your elders into a nursing home. This made sense when families lived together in close communities and had multiple generations in a home to share the duties. It is a lot harder to pull this off with children living farther apart, everyone working in full-time jobs outside the home, and parents living longer with heavier multiyear care more common now.

There was a Pakistani doctor who lived in their apartment building, and we owe her such a debt of gratitude. She would routinely check in on my parents, showing up even at 2:00 a.m. if there was a call from my mother asking for help. When an acute situation arose, though, it was all hands on deck.

My dad needed a cane to help steady his walk, but he hated using it—a sign of his wanting to be independent and strong, I suppose, to not give in to age and illness. So there was a constant battle between him and the caregivers. "Please use your cane" or "What will happen if you fall?" they'd ask, but he was resistant. And so the day came when he fell and broke his femur, requiring surgery and a whole array of decisions to be made. He ended up recovering well, and the surgeon was shocked at how quickly his bone had healed.

But it was a long road to get there. My brother from Melbourne and I flew back to Malaysia, and the next few weeks were spent taking turns in the hospital and at home managing Dad's care, Mum's concern and helplessness, and the many elements that come with a crisis. Then there were the doctors—so many of them—orthopedic surgeon, anesthesiologist, neurologist, pain specialist, geriatrician, rounding physicians in the ward, primary care physician, physical therapist, psychiatrist, and perhaps others I cannot remember now. Somehow in the healthcare system—whether in Malaysia or the US, it feels the same—even when the individuals are competent and caring, there is no one person managing the whole situation, the whole of the patient's return to health. For us, it was a round-robin of making sure each person on the healthcare team knew what the other was thinking and doing.

One day in the hospital, a family member who was visiting looked at my father's feet and wondered why they were red. Nurses had come and gone, doing their tasks but not observing much beyond their specific activity. It turned out the redness on his feet indicated a serious allergic reaction to one of the pain medications. These things might seem small in themselves, but they added to the emotional burden and exhaustion of the family because we were not trained for any of it and operating with very little sleep and extreme stress.

As Dad recovered from the surgery, his discharge from the hospital became the next question to be managed. Malaysia does not have rehabilitation centers as in the US. But Dad would need a high level of care for a while, as he would be bed-ridden for weeks, or even months. We didn't know how long it would be. I had to replicate a rehab setting in their home. The next few days were a blur of activity as I figured out what would be needed and got it into place. I found a hospital supply store in town and went to explore bed options; that seemed like a good place to start. The Chinese family that ran the store were so sympathetic and helpful, it made me cry. Being seen and feeling kindness from strangers is incredible. It is a lesson I still carry with me—it is free to be kind to someone.

In a few short days, a hospital bed, oxygen tanks, an anti-bedsore mattress, and all kinds of supplies I had never known even existed were delivered to the house and we were ready for the patient to be brought home. But the bigger question to be solved was how to provide round-the-clock nursing care and supervision.

We managed to set up home nursing care with nurses ro-tating through eight-hour shifts. This service is not sophisti-cated or regulated, and the level of care and professionalism varied greatly by individual. In addition, having strangers in your home all day and night is itself hugely stressful. For a lot of the time, I worried about how to leave my parents in this situation. I was barely managing to check in with my job and my team back home in the US. Their kindness in taking care of things and giving me the space to focus on my parents was incredible, but I had responsibilities and a career that deserved my attention.

Relief came from an unexpected source. A student, Bilkis, who had been set on her path to a PhD by my parents, moved in with them and took on the primary caregiver role. I barely knew her then but accepted her help gratefully—more on accepting help later—and have a lifelong debt to her for that incredible gift. She was a much better caregiver than I could ever be—calm, strong, capable, kind—and I truly admire her. Bilkis stayed for over a month in my parents' home, giving selflessly, working through all the decisions, and giving us siblings relief beyond measure. She was an angel in human form.

THE HYBRID MODEL

As shown by the story Shabnam just shared, most people just cannot take on full-time care for their aging loved ones. We have career obligations and children to care for. We may live in a different state or different country from our parents. In these cases, we have to outsource care. This leads to somewhat of a hybrid model where a primary caregiver is supported by an extended care team. This typically requires a care plan and team of facility workers, family members, friends, and neighbors. It gets you the care you need for everyone.

Shari

I ended up with a hybrid model. This meant some caregiving activities were owned by me, some by my siblings, and others were covered by staff at the assisted care facility where my father lived. When I was traveling, I would ask family, friends, or neighbors to help with my children, and my sister, along with the facility team where my dad lived, would help with my dad. To make this work, I had to have a care plan, scheduling my dad's day alongside my family's. Part of the time, my husband was active duty in the military and frequently forward deployed, which meant he had to travel to specific areas where his expertise was needed, sometimes staying for long periods of time. My job required travel to the other side of the US and internationally, as we had over fifty offices, so I would take red-eye flights and try to minimize my time away to support the schedule. While it worked in the short run, it was exhausting.

My care plan started with my dad's preferred schedule. He liked to wake up at 7:00 a.m. each day and needed help dressing and getting ready, which was minimal at first. As things progressed, his needs obviously changed, and since he was in assisted living, I scheduled the staff to wake him or make sure to take him to breakfast if he wasn't already up. My dad had always been an early riser, though as the years progressed, he would sleep later and sometimes miss breakfast. Then I would schedule daily activities, lunch, rest, and free time; often he would take a whittling kit outside with wood and create canes and walking sticks that we would sell at the local farmers' market. Then he would get ready for dinner, go down to get help with his meds, and I would come over with the kids to play Rummikub in the evening. If I wasn't traveling, I would pick him up in the late afternoon and he would ride with me to the kids' activities before dinner.

When I was traveling, I scheduled him to attend activities or outings with the assisted care staff. When he had downtime, he usually rested, socialized, or whittled. I kept in touch with him via his mobile phone or with the staff.

He also met a friend named Olive, a spunky resident who

was about ten years his senior but sharp as could be. She was wonderful, helping to run my dad's schedule, keeping him active, and just being a terrific companion for him. She had great stories; so many of the residents did, I loved listening to them talk about their lives. This worked well until Covid hit and I wasn't able to visit in person to see how things were going. Olive was a godsend during this time. It was also during this time that his condition started to deteriorate, and so did Olive's.

At first my dad was fairly independent and needed limited care, mostly just someone to prompt him to remember to take his medicine. He was even doing his own laundry. But then I started to notice small changes; for example, he forgot to take his eye drops and the bottles slowly accumulated in the fridge. Sometimes he would be wearing dirty clothes or in many cases could not locate his dentures. I also noticed that many of the soaps and toiletries went unused. When we went for a medical checkup, his blood pressure was unusually high and his macular degeneration pressures were off. That meant he needed to start getting help with his medications, and while we were at it, my sister added someone to help with laundry and a few other services. By this time, he was completely dependent on his walker. Luckily, Olive used one too, so she was excellent at making sure he did not leave his room without it.

As time passed, he needed prompting for meals. Sometimes with dementia, patients become confused about what is day and what is night. The schedule also required flexibility and grace, as some days he was just tired and wanted to rest. I did find having a consistent and preset schedule helped me plan, and it also reduced stress for him and gave him a sense of purpose. I highly recommend setting up a schedule and making sure everyone on the care team is aware of it. I also got to know everyone at his care facility, from the aides to the nurses to the dining and front-desk staff. If I could not reach my dad, I had plenty of people to call for help.

CARING FOR THE WHOLE PERSON

When we think of caregiving, we tend to focus on the basics, such as treating any medical issues and organizing the daily routines and safety needs of a parent. But it is just as important to care for the emotional and psychological needs of your loved one. What gives them joy and a good quality of life? How can you fulfill their wishes in terms of living a full and meaningful life until the end of their days?

In today's society, we sadly see older people being discounted and made invisible. They often are made to feel as if they do not have value to society and are a burden because they might not be actively giving back in some way. But the measure of a person is not in their productivity or income. It is in the wisdom and intangible human value they provide to us. So, when caregiving, remember to seek ways to enhance the quality of life of the parent as best you can. Even small ways of recognizing their skills and experience and fostering connections can be of great meaning.

Shabnam

When my father was about eighty-five and had been away from his teaching for six years, he felt depressed and sad at not being on campus and surrounded by students and faculty. He felt the joy in his life had been taken away by Parkinson's, and the days dragged with monotony. He just wanted to teach.

I felt terrible watching him yearn to be back in his happiest place, a university campus.

So I persuaded his university to hold a recognition event for my father. It was to be a way to celebrate his fifty years of teaching as a service to the country. The program turned out to be grander than we could have imagined, with over a hundred people attending. There were banners all over the university and lovely testimonial speeches presented by my father's students and mentees; it was a celebration of his great contribution to the field of teaching and English literature as well as a testament to how academia lifts up communities. Seeing my father's eyes light up at seeing his colleagues and students was priceless. He was feted, he was shown respect and applauded, and it was magnificent. He arrived in a wheelchair and people knelt down to kiss his hand and greet him in an ultimate form of respect. I could not have felt happier at giving my father a moment of glory and seeing him receive the love and admiration of so many people; it boosted his spirits and mine for a long time.

Because of that wonderful event, I learned that caregiving is not just about taking care of physical needs but also taking time for the real soul-enriching possibilities that raise people up and create lasting memories. Caregiving can help not just extend life but elevate it, surrounding everyone involved with joy.

CHAPTER TAKEAWAYS

A main takeaway from this chapter is that you cannot and should not try to do it all by yourself. When you are realistic and intentional about what you can do on your own and where you will need help, you can begin to create a care plan that works for everyone involved. This means setting up and cultivating partnerships, whether with your spouse or siblings or healthcare professionals.

To begin, make a list of all the kinds of care your loved one requires and another list of all the people in your care circle. Think about whose expertise fits where, how to work with them effectively, and ways to organize yourself to keep track of responsibilities and expectations. Having clear communication and periodic check-ins can greatly improve understanding and care delivery. Accepting help is important, but asking for help is even more important. Give yourself the grace of not being too shy to admit you are stressed or overwhelmed, and that it is natural and reasonable when caregiving is tough. And ideally, build your care team well before you need it.

5

Self-Caregiving

Caregiving is a word that has two components: *care* and *giving*. This is worth thinking about because the giving part truly involves giving of oneself. Giving time, energy, resources, love, attention, focus, emotional support—all this can be totally depleting when done for stretches of time and under stressful conditions.

When we have busy periods at work, for example, we know there will be a break and things will normalize. We know we're going to get a paycheck and maybe rewards and recognition. But with caregiving, so much is unseen and unrewarded, and that can increase the burnout one feels. It can be hard work without immediate gratification, without accolades and celebration, without a light at the end of the tunnel. Isolation can also be a problem if you are handling caregiving without supportive people around and with little chance of delegating or taking time off.

Add to that the responsibility you might feel constantly and the sense of impending doom as parents get increasingly ill and dependent. For all these reasons, if you are the primary caregiver, and even if you are one of multiple caregivers, it is essential to take care of yourself. You have to sustain yourself to be able to provide care and not have your own health negatively affected. Just as we are taught on airplanes to put on your own oxygen mask before you assist others, we need to actively care for ourselves during our caregiving journey.

Self-care can mean different things for each of us, and you know best what replenishes your physical and mental energy. Basic self-care includes managing stress, getting enough sleep, and taking care of your own health by exercising and visiting doctors. Self-care can also involve creating boundaries at home and work so that you can balance each of your responsibilities. It may also look like joining support communities that share advice and resources about the challenges your loved one is facing. This is an empowering way to learn, reduce stress, and feel engaged with others in similar situations. Being validated in the caregiving journey is important, knowing that your efforts are meaningful and valued can give positive momentum to keep going.

It is a shame that caregiving is still an invisible job, not applauded as it should be; caregivers are true heroes and should be celebrated. Until that happens, though, it is up to us to keep self-care top of mind. You are your best advocate, so don't forget to keep yourself high on the priority list. It is easier said than done sometimes, but the downstream effects of recovery can be so traumatic and severe that it is much better to make a determined and conscious effort all through your caregiving period. You will be glad you didn't lose sight of your health and well-being along the way.

Self-care should be just as much of a component of caregiving as talking to loved ones' doctors or managing their financials. It is that important. This chapter explores a few aspects of self-care that caregivers should be aware of and shares stories about our challenges with this topic.

UNDERSTANDING BURNOUT

Caregiving takes a toll on people in different ways, and it is important to understand these so you can better take care of yourself along the way. Caregiving can be stressful because there are sometimes urgent and important decisions to be made and changes to implement, but caregiving can also cause burnout from the sheer exhaustion of keeping so many balls in the air for extended periods of time. WebMD provides a good distinction of stress versus burnout. Burnout is "a form of exhaustion caused by constantly feeling swamped. It happens when we experience too much emotional, physical, and mental fatigue for too long. . . . Stress can make you feel overwhelmed, but burnout makes you feel depleted and used up. . . . Burnout . . . makes you feel hopeless, cynical, and resentful."

Recognizing the signs and symptoms of burnout—such as low motivation, reduced productivity at work, or getting sick often—are important so you can make adjustments and get back to a more healthful state. There is no magic trick for burnout, but there are steps you can take to help reduce it, such as getting sleep and exercise, eating healthy food, and asking for help to reduce your own workload. It is critical to catch burn-out early so that you can continue to be an effective caregiver while also protecting your own health and well-being.

Shari

Caregiving is some of the hardest work you will do. And as I have said before, I would not trade it for anything, but as a people pleaser I tried to do it all—career, children, marriage, caregiving—without much help. Remember that you are also living a life, and that your happiness is worth as much as that of those you are caring for. You must find balance, so give yourself grace and practice self-care. It does not mean you are selfish.

As I write this, I am just coming off a yearlong break. Yes, you read that correctly, a yearlong break. After raising my family, caregiving, working, losing my dad, and diving deeper into work, I woke up one day to realize I was completely sepa-rated from myself. I had been trained to move at such a clip, I did not know any other speed, and I couldn't go on any longer.

My body was exhausted. Though it had performed sol-idly and diligently for years, now it needed a break. I felt this incredible sense of dread daily. I could barely lift my right leg because of a hip issue; I'm a lifelong runner and years of pounding the pavement had taken their toll on me. I looked at my beautiful kids—grown up and starting their own lives—and wondered if they would miss me when I was gone because I just couldn't see the future. I was physically and mentally ex-hausted, but I had no idea what a break was or even how to have one. So I started to hash out a plan. I knew in order to be the Ya Ya—which is what my future grandkids will call me—I dreamed of being and living the retired life my husband and I had always talked about, I needed to make some big changes. And I needed to make them now. My goals were to heal my body, to find peace in my mind, and to reconnect with myself.

What happened to me is what happens to so many women and caregivers. We give and give until we have given so much, we are completely burned out and can no longer remember who we are or what our purpose in life is. For me, it was very hard to think about what I should have been doing for myself because I had lost myself along the way and had no boundaries. When I look back, the signs had been there for a while.

For instance, I had more than just one major fall: In the spring of 2018, my travel schedule was intense, and while home one weekend, I had a mountain bike accident. At the end of that same year of global travel and my husband retiring from the military, I fell off a ladder and cracked my head open while hanging Christmas lights because I just wanted it done and did not want to ask for help. In 2022, after my dad's celebration of life, I took a spill in a park. In 2023, I stepped off the deck, hoping to fetch the dog, but fell, landing on my wrist and shattering it, which required surgery. I was a mess.

DEALING WITH GUILT

One aspect that many caregivers say they experience and which adds to the challenges of caregiving is guilt. If you never feel like you are doing enough for your loved one, it can eat away at you and harm your emotional well-being. This low level of anxiety activates your body's threat response, depleting your energy and driving poor decisions.

A core part of daily self-care should help you mentally get back to a positive baseline. You need to be able to begin each day with a full cup, meaning you feel that you can effectively accomplish tasks that need to get done. Approaches such as meditation and exercise can help—and these can look different for everyone. This can be a formal seated meditation practice, or your meditation could be doing the dishes without any interruption while listening to your favorite musical artist and singing along. Your exercise could be a sweaty hour of lifting weights at the gym or a contemplative walk around a nature preserve. Find what works for you and then schedule it in. Don't give yourself a chance to skip or forget your daily self-care.

Self-compassion is another excellent practice. It is as easy as reminding yourself that even though things are not perfect, they are good enough. You, just like everyone else, have limitations. Be kind to yourself. Focus on all that you are doing—reward yourself for the service you are providing for your loved one and the role modeling you are doing for others. When milestones occur, it is okay to pat yourself on the back for a job well done.

Shabnam

One great form of self-care is engaging with others who share your journey. Regardless of the diagnosis your parent is facing, there is likely a support group that can provide advice, resources, and a community, and this can be a useful place to get yourself organized to do your task better but also to gain moral support.

If you have a family member with Alzheimer's, for example, find a community of caregivers and learn from others about how to take care of yourself emotionally. I joined online support groups through the Alzheimer's Association, and also met with people in Malaysia through my high school network who were dealing with a similar situation. I learned many useful techniques, including activities for keeping a parent occupied in a positive way and effective ways to communicate. Everything was tailored to the diagnosis, coming from people who had already been through it.

It gave me such a sense of relief and sanity to be with others who were facing the same challenges and working on solutions day-to-day. It helped me find energy and courage, as we could all share our stories and that feeling of not being able to do more or make things magically better. There was a quiet acceptance of the challenge, and just knowing that I was not missing anything obvious was calming. Feeling better equipped to manage your responsibilities is essential for self-care because it reduces stress and builds a feeling of satisfaction and control.

THE EFFECTS OF STRESS

By now we all know stress is not always good for us, especially when it is chronic and unmanaged. Over half of US adults say stress has negatively affected their behavior. So when you add caregiving into your already complicated life, the impact can be catastrophic.

And it affects everyone differently. From your cardiovascular, musculoskeletal, and digestive systems to skin and hair to mood and emotions, nothing is left out. We also store stress in our bodies, so while we may not notice it at the time of the initial stressor, our bodies are keeping track and can express physical distress at a later date with a variety of different issues. Mentally, stress can cause behavior changes, cognitive delays, or memory loss that makes decision-making challenging. It also causes overall anxiety, irritability, and trouble sleeping.

It can be difficult to notice the gradual impacts of stress on the body. But these small physiological changes that happen in the nervous system and brain add up over time. There is more research being done about adrenal fatigue and how stress triggers hormones such as cortisol in the body. Many of us wander, trip, or charge through life ignoring these signs just to get one more thing done. The other issue is ignoring stress, which is a pervasive issue in our society. For example, over two-thirds of US adults have a digestive issue of some type—a common side effect of stress—but most don't seek medical help for it.

Sure, I'm stressed, you might think, *but I have to get things done.* You may not feel you have time to unpack stress or do stress-relieving activities, but the more you bottle it up, the more of an issue it can become over time, leading to physical or mental challenges that you can no longer ignore. The biggest thing you can do for yourself is to admit you are stressed. Once you admit you are stressed, finding ways to address it becomes much easier. My suggestions are breathwork, spiraling out of negative talk, rest, and focusing on eating the right foods. If you want to start with two things, then sleep and breaking up negative talk will make a huge difference.

Shari

There is much stress and uncertainty when caregiving, which led me to being overwhelmed and caused me to be constantly in fight mode. For me, this expressed itself in a couple of key ways. First, I was constantly planning. I rarely enjoyed the present because I was always moving on to the next thing. Also, I had lost a connection with my body. This caused my digestion to be a challenge. I had IBS-C and ulcerative colitis. My gut was in such bad shape that I was having yearly colonoscopies, taking steroids, and ballooning up every time I ate something. When I was working with a therapist, after ignoring stress for some time, I told her that I had spent more than twenty years dealing with gut issues. She promptly informed me that most of her patients had gut issues of some sort. Only further validating for me the connection between the mind and gut.

I was very stressed and just could not relax, no matter how hard I tried. The bigger issue was that I did not realize this until after my dad had passed and I finally had the opportunity to reset myself after leaving my job. One of the challenges of stress is when you are in it, it is often hard to see or feel as you are making it happen and don't give yourself a chance to take a break or come up for air.

My body had been keeping score. It was time to, as my husband repeatedly told me, take a moment and heal. My time off helped me find myself, fix my gut, fix my hip, get in touch with my body, reconnect with my family, and prioritize what was important. And I did it. It took lots and lots of work, but I was dedicated and had the ability to do it.

My advice is to be prepared for uncertainty, as that is the true reality. Celebrate when you have some consistency and do all you can to avoid losing touch with yourself. When your inner voice says, *Get help,* do what you can to get it and find a way to keep that mindful practice going. For me, this started with meditation during the first year of the Covid pandemic, as a way to center myself in a world of absolute uncertainty. I started meditating and doing restorative yoga for five to fifteen minutes a day. Then I expanded into hypnotherapy, targeting my vagus nerve to address my gut issues. If you are having gut issues, see a doctor, a gastrointestinal specialist, and a therapist. The thing that really helped me was realizing it was not the food I was eating that was causing me problems but instead my nervous system in constant fight mode.

I had one of the worst colonoscopy results I have ever had during the first month of my year off. I started having them regularly when our daughter was two; she is now twenty-two. So this had been going on for a very long time. After the colonoscopy, my new GI doctor told me the inflammation in my colon was very bad and, overall, I was headed down the wrong path. He told me I had two choices: make big changes or prepare for Crohn's and colon cancer.

I opted for option one and immediately stopped drinking alcohol and started hypnotherapy and doing the work. It was a game changer for me but also opened me up to see how my lifestyle had driven me to this point. I had neglected the one thing I should cherish: me! I also started physical therapy for my hip and did over 130 sessions to get my strength back. I met an incredible group of women who were in the same place as me, and we started to find strength and resilience in each other. Over time I started realizing I had always been strong—to be a caregiver you have to be—but I was lost. Like many lost things, you can be found; but it takes good solid work, the power of community, and commitment.

My mindful practice is now daily. It varies and includes meditation, breathwork, Reiki, and lifting at the gym. I also love the water and find so much peace when I am around it. The hard conversation for me was really with myself, admitting that I was at capacity and needed help. At the time I didn't know why I could not have the conversation, but now I know I was afraid of not being enough. I had come to define myself in my utility, my ability to take on so much and come out fine and on top. Now I realize what I was doing was not scalable, and if I had just stopped and accepted I was in over my head, maybe, just maybe, I would have been able to see that and adjust.

Shabnam

Being strong during the last two years of caregiving for my father took a lot out of me, but I did not realize it then. I just kept going because I needed to and because I felt I was invincible. A hero complex can be a very dangerous thing at any time. I didn't think about me; all my energy was spent on keeping the balls of work, children, parents, and spouse in the air. I was stressed all the time, felt behind all the time, and felt guilty all the time for not doing any of those things to my liking and satisfaction. It was crazy how much pressure I was putting on myself.

What I did not realize then is that stress is cumulative. Even though you may not be stopped in the moment by any one stressor, each one weakens you like small cracks in a dam, especially if you don't do anything to rebuild yourself. At some point, the wall is not going to hold anymore.

In the last few weeks with my father, I was extremely stressed, practically living at the hospital and dreading the inevitable outcome. I knew it was the end for him, but I didn't want to admit it. I was scared. I fought his end beyond what was reasonable.

After his funeral I flew back to the US in a strange state of limbo, not quite shifting gears and yet feeling like the adrenaline and then absence of adrenaline was hard to explain to anyone. One day, I woke up with both my hands completely numb; I could not even pick up my phone. I was puzzled, confused, and scared. What was this? It happened for several days until I finally started seeing doctors, who gave me lots of tests and yet no diagnosis other than stress.

Then, another day, I woke up with screaming pain in both feet. I freaked out, not knowing what was going on. I could not put my feet on the ground; I could not walk without excruciating pain. I was diagnosed as having plantar fasciitis in both feet, something that, again, can be attributed to stress. It took me two years of going to every kind of doctor to be able to walk without pain. To this day I struggle. I saw chiropractors, got steroid shots, did acupuncture, got orthotics made, did physical therapy. It was one full year of pain so bad that I'd question whether what should be a simple trip to the grocery store was worth the effort. Stress is a crazy thing.

I believe the stress of those caregiving years had accumulated in my body and was finally unleashed when my father passed away and I stopped constantly moving. Could I have lessened the health impact of my caregiving journey? Very likely, and that is what every caregiver should think about doing in the moment. Protect your health intentionally. You need to be strong and healthy both during and after your caregiving.

My health issues also made going back into the workforce difficult. I started a new job at a biotech company but had to hide the fact that my feet were in extreme pain from days of travel and office work in formal shoes. I have a high tolerance for pain, but it took so much energy to constantly tune it out that sometimes I could not think straight. Pain is interesting, too, because it is often invisible to others. So you have to take care of yourself because others will not know what you are enduring. Be your own advocate, give yourself grace, think of yourself as a whole person, and take care of yourself.

CHAPTER TAKEAWAYS

Forgetting to prioritize one's own care during the process of caregiving (and balancing all your other responsibilities) is a recipe for trouble. Marriages suffer, performance at work suffers, people suffer. There is always an endless juggling of tasks and always too little time. But neglecting your own health and well-being can be disastrous all around. At the end of the day, your health is a core component of keeping all those balls in the air. If you become ill or disabled in some way, that can negatively affect your own life goals as well as your caregiving goals.

So keep yourself and your well-being at the top of your priorities and give time, space, and attention to yourself as well as to those you are caring for. This may not look consistent, as you will have good stretches and bad stretches, but what is important is not losing yourself in the process and always remembering to come back and reset. Carve out pockets of time and escape so you can really go off duty and recharge yourself.

Only you can do this for yourself, and it will keep you from falling apart from the arduous toll that caregiving can take. Self-care can also be a big positive for everyone around you, as you will put less stress on them and they will not feel stress seeing you heading down a dangerous path. When we neglect ourselves, it might feel heroic in the moment, but it always has negative consequences in the long run. Help others help you. Ask for help, accept the generosity of others, and let others into your world of caregiving so they can support you. You are the gatekeeper for all the sources that can sustain and nourish you during caregiving.

6

Managing Career and Caregiving

Having a job means steady income, health benefits, security, and belonging to a social unit, but when you add caregiving, it means balancing, juggling, and integrating many new aspects into your life. If you are one of the many caregivers who also has a paid job and/or a career you are passionate about, you will need to figure out how to manage both sets of responsibilities, which can be challenging at times. For many of us, working while caregiving is not optional. Others may prioritize caregiving by choice or necessity for a period of time, which comes with its own complications, such as how to off-ramp from your job, manage without income for a period, and potentially on-ramp back to a job or career if you choose.

Caregivers are getting younger and younger as baby boomers age and live longer. But at the same time, chronic health issues are on the rise, meaning parents and other retiree-age loved ones need more care. Don't despair, though: Let's first look at some of the facts so you can see you are not alone.

The global workforce is about 3.6 billion people, or 40 percent of the global population, according to Statista. In the US alone, the Bureau of Labor Statistics reports the civilian labor force is over 170 million. Many of us today rely on at least one income, if not two, to support our families and life-styles. Another interesting fact reported by AARP is, of the US workforce, about 53 million are unpaid caregivers, the economic value equaling a staggering $600 billion. The other fact is 22 percent of those unpaid caregivers also work full-time. Juggling family, work, and caregiving is a breeding ground for stress and burnout. This is part of why self-care has become a very important topic for many Generation X and millennials.

Most employers today do not have adequate programs to support someone who is going through a caregiving experience. They have concierge benefits to help you find care, such as Care.com, which is helpful to fill the gap if you need temporary help. Some employers also provide an Employee Assistance Program (EAP), which has tools for managing your own mental and physical health but rarely has a comprehensive set of support for helping you manage eldercare.

Work can be both a welcome distraction and a further inducer of stress. But many people carry fear around being vulnerable at work. They don't want to share the truth about their caregiving situation, as they feel it may show weakness. For women, this becomes sadly amplified because we don't need one more thing working against us in most cases.

Employer assistance is also lacking when it comes to the pain of loss, which is often an end result of caregiving for parents. Workplace grief experts note that our response to death, especially in the workforce, could use some improvement. Caregiving situations don't always result in death, but even when employers have assistance programs, they are limited in scope and duration. These are inadequate for the employee; you can't put a specific date and time on grief.

It is not a secret that while you are caregiving and working, your productivity could be affected, and about 27 percent of caregivers move to part-time or stop working for a period of time, as stated in the S&P Global report on caregiving. Many turn down promotions or make the decision to leave work.

In this chapter, we will discuss the facts about unpaid caregivers and the process for thinking through how to manage caregiving, your family, and your career. We offer suggestions about options and discuss the reality that most of us face when it comes to our jobs. We share our decisions to leave our jobs and the pros and cons that resulted. The goal is to give you some insight on what to take into consideration when making choices around your career and caregiving. It is important to acknowledge there are many variables involved in this decision, and we will provide a framework to help you decide on the best answer for yourself.

TO QUIT OR NOT TO QUIT

Shabnam

In 2017, I decided to leave my job and focus full-time on

caregiving. It was a big decision for me, but I am so glad I made it. In hindsight, I even wonder if I should have stopped working one year before I did. It would have saved me a lot of stress and downstream personal health issues. It would have also reduced stress for my parents, my husband and children, my work team, and the on-site caregivers of my parents. But I did not realize that at the time and kept focused on doing (or trying to do) everything for everybody.

Between parent care, family duties, and work obligations, I wonder how I survived. Crises with my parents happened every few months in Malaysia, requiring me to drop everything at work and fly off halfway across the world. As a friend and fellow caregiver said to me recently, "We were only doing 80 percent of each of those jobs," so no wonder everything suffered. But doing those three things at 80 percent each still adds up to more than one human can sustain, especially if it is under pressure and constant mental and physical exhaustion.

As a senior executive in a pharmaceutical company, I was responsible for running a team of a hundred people in a patient services business segment. I traveled around the country to do fieldwork as well as attend conferences, which meant a very packed agenda all the time. So when I had to head home to Malaysia to take care of my parents, it meant rearranging project deliverables, having others cover for me, explaining my absence for two to three weeks at a time, and generally leaning on many people to make do and take on extra work on my behalf. For a year and a half I did this, bouncing back and forth when my parents needed me. As I was the primary caregiver, there was no alternative.

Fortunately, I had an amazing team, and especially my

Japanese colleagues and senior management were incredibly kind and supportive. But there was still pressure to deliver on business goals, and I wanted to meet my obligations. I sat in some hospital or another in Kuala Lumpur multiple times, working on budgets and operational goals and barely keeping it together. The stress was horrible, and as a driven, type A person with a track record of doing quality work, the conditions were a perfect setup to make me feel inadequate when I could not give my full effort to work and deliver at the caliber I expected of myself. It was a no-win situation.

Finally, after several of these back-and-forth trips in crisis mode, I decided it was impossible to sustain. When my father could no longer swallow food due to his Parkinson's and required a feeding tube—which he routinely pulled out, as he did not want to live that way—I decided to leave my job. It was the right thing to do, even though I did not know then that I would never go back to that track of pharmaceutical management. I am so fortunate that I was able to quit. I was able to spend more time in Malaysia directly caring for my parents, and I was present for the final months before my father passed away. Being there in person took away the guilt and regret that I would otherwise have felt for the rest of my life. It was a blessing in disguise, even though it meant off-ramping from a career track that I had worked so hard to build.

Shari

Life is short but wide, and during that time we are blessed with many, many lessons. Some easy, some hard, and some just no-brainers. Like, if you are tired, then sleep. Easy, right? Well, not always. When I hit my breaking point, it was really a breaking point for me. I knew I had to change or it was going to do me in. I had fallen, twisted, or broken something multiple times in the past several years. This was not normal. Although prone to getting myself into some crazy situations, this was really more than usual. My dentist, who was a close friend, saw me more for mishaps than social visits, it seemed.

The last injury, requiring surgery for my wrist, was the final draw for me. I had to step away and truly address what was going on. My thoughts had turned darker than usual, and my work environment had become so toxic it was dreadful. I started tuning in and focusing more on spiritual practices like manifesting, meditation, and listening to my body. This took me some time to develop, but despite my track record of not giving myself credit for my accomplishments, I began doing what I could to make up for years of not listening.

During the first year of the Covid pandemic, I found meditation and restorative yoga to be sources of peace to calm a nervous system in full fight mode. And when a young man who worked for me took his own life, this practice was about the only thing I could do to calm myself. For years, I had felt I could not pause or step away, because I couldn't let all these people down. I had a global team of over two hundred people, and they were some of the best. When I had issues with my dad, like when he fell, they always stepped in and stepped up. It was incredible, and I felt so supported.

When my father passed away, we left the house for a few days and went to Montana. We needed time to reflect in the Big Sky Country, our happy place. When we came home, our house was full of flowers, food, cards, and kindness. So much compassion and kindness from people I worked with, people I worked for, and our incredible friend group. What I realize now is when you don't give yourself time to recover, you lose yourself and then you are no good to anyone. After years of just pushing through, my armor was rock-solid and my heart almost closed to visitors. This was the only response holding me back from the pain.

After losing my dad, I had to look very closely at the areas of my life that I had been actively neglecting and tried the bottom-up and top-down approaches to fixing them. I recognized one great source of stress was my job.

While my support network was solid, I never shared my entire situation with the people I worked with or loved, so they didn't know that I had two, maybe three, full-time jobs—the one I worked with them, my role as a mom, and my caregiving. I was a woman in the C-suite and new to the industry. My responsibilities meant I had to travel frequently—exhausting in its own right. All this had me already feeling like I had a target on my back. That made me very apprehensive to share. I shared the most with my boss and team, but it was a safe, sanitized version, not the whole story. The only person who probably knows the entire story is my husband, as he had a front-row seat to everything. Though he tried to point out these issues and help when needed, he was also feeling the pain. I knew I had to leave the constant travel and perpetual busyness behind and hit pause.

After all of this, my exhaustion was at peak levels, but I had used all my bereavement leave after my dad passed away, and while I still felt empty inside, numb, I continued at a pace

I had come to know as normal. One particular week in June, shortly after my dad's celebration of life, I had back-to-back trips to the East Coast, and I decided to take red-eye flights for both. This meant I could spend time with my family, hop on a plane, sleep, work the full day, and then meet two of my very best friends who lived in New York for dinner before another full workday. If you have taken red-eyes, you know this was optimistic at best. I made it all the way to meeting my friends, but while walking to the restaurant, I slipped and hit my head on the curb and broke my two front teeth.

It was excruciatingly painful. Luckily, my girlfriends jumped into action and helped me locate a dentist—no easy feat at 6:00 p.m. in Manhattan. We ended up finding some-one who could put a temporary fix on my teeth. It took several hours and then I went back to my hotel. The next morning I was up bright and early for an earnings call back-to-back with a presentation to about one hundred women. Then I jumped back to work with my team on press and internal communi-cations post-earnings. I had composite material on my teeth, cuts on my face, and a golf-ball-size bump on my knee so swol-len I could barely walk. To say the least, I felt terrible.

I DoorDashed ice packs and got the first flight home, cry-ing most of the way. I was exhausted mentally and physically. This latest fall was my body telling me—again—to wake up. While I didn't take time to get counseling or take the break I really needed, this was a breakthrough for me. I realized I had to hatch the plan for my departure from my job, but I needed to make sure that it would be safe and comfortable for my family. As a family, we weren't in a position to have only one income, so I had to figure out how to do this. At the same time,

I knew that if I did not leave, my situation would not get any better, and I needed to prioritize myself so I could once again show up as the person I was and be true to that.

I spent the next couple of months thinking about the future, what I could do, and how I was going to do it. Work was so integrated into my life that it was challenging for me to see who I'd be without it. I asked the company to get me a coach, and I cried for the first few sessions, though she helped me get over my fear and put myself first. For years, I'd heard about people being exhausted and the bad things that happened to them. I finally realized that was me, and I needed to take the time to help myself and my family. I had conversations with my boss, sharing a list of what I needed and the timing, and I began my exit. I jumped full force into building my exit plan, and one year later, I was gone.

My coach also helped me find a doctor who took a benchmark of my health and got me back to being healthy again. In all honesty, I should have assessed my situation and stepped back earlier when I could feel I was slipping and my thoughts were turning darker than usual. When I was deep into caregiving mode, though, I didn't let myself feel pain, and when my husband pointed out his concerns, I shut him down.

If someone is telling you they are concerned about your health or stress level, listen to them. When you start to feel overwhelmed, pause, assess, and investigate. You are likely past where you need to be and you need to step away, take stock, and build a new path forward. You can get back to where you need to be, but you need to give yourself the grace and space to do it.

REINVENTING YOUR WORK SELF

If you have made changes to your job and career in order to focus on caregiving, there may come a point when you need to think about whether (or how) to return to your prior career track or find a new normal. The process of caregiving and loss and grief can fundamentally alter who you are and how you think about everything. It can be a similar process to having a first child with all the decisions around career and childcare that go along with that. However, when it comes to caregiving for elders, there are fewer resources available to support you through the decision-making and the execution of either path.

There are a few key things to think about. If you can, allow yourself time to heal and recover before jumping back into things. Find a way to change tracks because what worked for you before may not be the best fit for you now. Recognize that you may have a whole new perspective on what is important, and there is nothing wrong with rearranging your life to match these new priorities and your new self. If it gives you comfort to go back to exactly where you were before, that is okay too. There is no fixed answer to what is right. What is best for you will depend on the choices available to you, your financial flexibility, and your emotional and physical state. It is important to recognize that caregiving can come with a magnitude of change. For the sake of your future well-being, you must allow yourself space to return to or reinvent your work self.

Shabnam

In 2018, after my dad's funeral in Malaysia, I went home to the US and endured several months of being completely washed out from exhaustion and emotional overload. Then I got a call from my dear mentor and champion who had been CEO of a pharmaceutical company where I'd worked previously.

He had heard about my loss and wanted to help if he could. "We need to get you back to work," he said. "Why don't you go to a small company for a change? Call my buddy Gene and he will get you started on thinking about your next steps."

That call got me out of my funk, and for two wonderful years I worked at a start-up oncology biotech company. It felt strange but good. I was different, and so a different work setting was the best thing that could have happened to me. It was a perfect place, where I was surrounded by lovely people and a worthy mission that I was passionate about. That one call was pivotal for my recovery and getting back into the workforce, and I am blessed that my mentor understood I did not want to go back to the prior setting of a big pharmaceutical company. I had done enough time there and was ready for a bigger role in a smaller company with a fresh environment. If it had not been for off-ramping to take care of my parents, I might not have ended up in the biotech entrepreneurial mode, which ended up being fantastic for me.

So keep people who will make that call close to you. People who know you better than yourself, who will not shy away from pushing you to move forward and get back to thriving, are rare and precious. They take searching for and building a relationship with and nurturing. We should always be looking for those people, whether at work, at home, at play, or in other parts of life.

Starting back into working was almost a relief, as it gave me structure and belonging again, filling plenty of hours and using my mind in a way that required me to fully show up. Work seemed like play. With this new place and set of new people, I could create some distance from my recent experience—I could be someone untouched by grief and loss. I was productive, pretending that everything was okay, not even talking about what had happened or the impact it had had on my life and well-being. Sometimes I would feel guilty about having fun and being happy and silly, as if the weight of parent care had become a badge of honor and I should not shirk it. But I was needed by others, and the work was exciting and full of positive energy. We worked on bringing new cancer drugs into development.

I still had my mum to worry about, but as she was deep into her dementia, the task was actually easier and didn't take over my life. Fortunately, our helpers provided excellent love and care so I could be at ease. When one parent goes and the other is left on their own, it can be a very tricky period in eldercare; more questions arise about how and where caretaking will take place and who will be the primary caregiver. I had some relief from traveling back and forth to Malaysia because Mum was stable and there were no crises.

In many cases, there is a rearranging of living arrangements for the remaining parent, which can have career implications for the primary caregiver. Because so much of the time the primary caregiver is a woman, this means there is a huge impact on women's careers at this point. Men are increasingly entering this role and are also underserved, as caregiving is not seen as a male issue. I have countless peers who had to off-ramp like me or take career breaks—which really changes the trend line in terms of progression and financial growth. This crisis is increasing, as we have an aging population, but it has not entered the national dialogue nor been dealt with in terms of policy and corporate or societal problem-solving.

Since work had been such a large part of my identity and use of my brain ever since my college days—I had not taken any time off except for three months each time a child was born (and that can hardly be categorized as time off!)—when suddenly finding myself not working, not belonging to a team, not having a paycheck or deliverables or work travel, and not needing to show up onstage somewhere, it was incredibly dis-orienting. In addition to grieving my father, I was also griev-ing the loss of my entire routine and way of functioning. And while the two years prior had been full of responsibilities for Mum's and Dad's care, suddenly there was a void. I would wake up and feel I had to call and check in and do some im-portant things but then become conscious of the fact that all that was done. It was less a relief than a weird feeling of hav-ing forgotten something, an absence and confusion and lack of something else to turn to and channel my energy into. Getting back to a job was the best thing to happen to me. It was the therapy I needed to get back to a familiar self that was secure, so I could account for my time in a responsible way.

Before my parent care journey, my life was a neat and tidy puzzle made up of family, job, parents, household care, children's activities, and so on, and that was completely shattered when I went into full-time caregiving. I ended up losing my dad, my career track, my income, and my health. The new puzzle took two years to build, and it looked very different. Now, even more years later, I am so grateful to be in this new puzzle—more at ease with my place in life and my choices, more ready to grab life fully and give and get joy, much more powerful from knowing I did the right thing and gave it my all.

Without the choice to off-ramp from work, I probably would have stayed on that same treadmill and kept working in the same way for many years. Though I would have had more income and maybe a higher-level position in work, I would not by any means have had the influence, confidence, or peace of mind I have now. I am free of guilt and regret. What a blessing in hindsight. When I went back to work in a different way, I ended up making more in less hours, which I never would have thought possible. I also went back to school and started my board career, which will hopefully be fruitful for the next decade. The life connections and impact from being a resource to others are immensely satisfying.

In addition, working with Shari on this book, for a common goal, has been a cathartic way to process all that happened. The process of taking our difficult journeys and morphing them into a resource for others has made me realize that I wrongly measured my self-worth in terms of dollars—how limited and inaccurate! Our self-worth comes from generating goodwill, not cash. Caregiving generates goodwill in spades and is a worthy endeavor.

CHAPTER TAKEAWAYS

When you are balancing a career and raising a family or dealing with other responsibilities, caregiving being added on top can upset the rhythm and leave you feeling overwhelmed. The potential of stepping away from your job needs to be carefully thought through for financial reasons and personal well-being. As a society we are slowly starting to lift the stigma on caregiving breaks from a job, but there are no sureties or specific protections in place. While the answer is unique to the situation, giving all your options consideration is definitely worth the time.

If you are juggling a career and caregiving and you are considering leaving work, begin with the objective facts. Write down the pros and cons of leaving or staying at your job. Get advice from doctors, financial advisers, family, and colleagues. Align with stakeholders, and don't operate in a vacuum, because others are also affected. Make sure *you* are included in your list of priorities.

Here are a few questions to think about:

1. Can you afford to leave work? Depending on the situation, sometimes you can use short-term or long-term disability leave. Also, consider whether your company has an EAP and look into the Family and Medical Leave Act. What is the state of your backup finances?
2. Can you afford mentally *not* to leave work? Consider first the impact on your health and well-being. Honestly assess where you are at right

now, and where you will be in six months to a
year if you stay on the same trajectory. Not being
available to your loved ones due to work obligations might later have a deep emotional impact,
leading to feelings of guilt and regret.

3.   What would the process of off-ramping look like?
How will you minimize risk and uncertainty
while downsizing career and finances? Take stock
of your assets. Determine what, if any, of your
loved one's assets can go toward their care. If
there are not any assets, how will you and other
caregivers pay for what is needed? Assume the
worst and plan ahead.

Whatever you decide, take the time to make peace with
it all. For many of us, work is our identity, a key part of our
social fabric, the sole source of our financial security, and our
day-to-day routine. You will grieve it and possibly feel resentment when and if you leave. Try to come to peace with this as
soon as possible so you do not carry this resentment forward.
Do not let it become a poison in your body, as it will influence
your health and your ability to be a good caregiver. Remember
why you are doing this. While it will be hard, caregiving for a
loved one can also be a beautiful life experience.

INTERLUDE

Caregiving Across Cultures and Countries

Shabnam

The year before my dad passed away was perhaps the most difficult one. Mum was no longer able to run the household and take care of Dad's care; Dad was rapidly losing control of his body and becoming depressed from being able to comprehend all the loneliness and lack of joy that came with it. Meanwhile, I was halfway across the world juggling teenagers and work and the cultural baggage of being the daughter who had abandoned her parents after having run off to America and married outside her religious and cultural boundaries.

When we enter caregiving, we bring a variety of assumptions, expectations, and biases to the task. The way we were raised, the religious and cultural norms that have shaped our worldview, our socioeconomic backgrounds, as well as our place of origin are all significant. All this background shapes how we think about caregiving and how we go about the task itself. This matters because all these various factors can be at odds with the perspectives of our parents and the other stakeholders in our caregiving journey.

And yet, taking care of our parents and elders is a fundamental responsibility that we share quite universally across the globe, regardless of location, religion, social status, or demographics. It is a societal value viewed with respect and admiration. It is "the right thing to do." The act of serving our elders in their time of need completes the cycle of life, as very often these same people have taken care of bearing and raising and nurturing us at the beginning of our lives. But humans are complicated and life is messy, and so many factors come into play when we think about caregiving.

For example, perhaps your parents come from a culture where there is a strong preference against nursing homes (as there is in much of Asia and among Asians who have moved to the US), as mine did. It is the worst possible thing a child can do, cruel to the parent and signaling a complete breakdown of the whole contract between parent and child. This is still the case in many parts of Asia, but in our modern world this is becoming harder and harder to achieve and that adds stress to caregiving.

Add to that a further challenge if you live somewhere where you do not have the same access to support and paid caregivers and therefore cannot afford to keep your parents at home when they require heavy care. Asians who live in the US can get caught in a bind when culture clashes with what is practical and possible. Only those who can afford to pay for caregivers in the home and make renovations to their houses to allow wheelchair access and other modifications can keep their parents at home, but this is as rare as it is costly.

As a generalization, elders who value independence and privacy will fight to live on their own, even when they cannot fully do so safely or well. On the other hand, in some cultures, the idea of living on one's own at the end of life is a sign of failure for the family, a breakdown of cultural values that emphasize the importance of directly caring for parents in their time of need.

Co-locating elders closer to the primary caregiver can alleviate a lot of issues, but it can also be disruptive to the elder, taking away some quality of life (familiarity, friends, independence). A more mobile population means that very often we are not living in proximity to our parents, and there are implications for what happens downstream. There are beautiful examples of adult children moving their parents in to live with them so they can be very present and directly in contact much of the time. But many people have jobs and commitments that do not enable them to do this, and we need to be free of judgment about the choices they make. Some of these decisions are outside our control (what healthcare options are available), and some are choices we make (should we move our parents to live closer to us).

Spouses and partners who come from different cultural backgrounds sometimes struggle to agree on decisions around caregiving for parents. Marriages break up when there is a major difference in cultural backgrounds without a mechanism for working out a caregiving plan that is acceptable to everyone. Decisions on how to allocate finances and personal time can also be a source of conflict if there isn't a common basis for thinking about caregiving. With more couples both working outside the home, there is also less caregiving capacity available.

In Japan, where longevity is extremely high and people are living well into their nineties and beyond, there is a crisis of care already. There are not enough young people to take care of the elderly; hence, the advanced use of robots in nursing homes compared to other countries. Because the government plays such a big role in providing healthcare and basic care in Japan, the experience is radically different. A case manager is assigned the moment it becomes apparent that a medical condition is going to require a care approach. That case manager remains with that person until their end of life, acting as an advocate and manager of both healthcare and all associated living needs. From identifying suitable living accommodations to ensuring doctors' visits and transitions between settings of care, the elder is never left to figure out things on their own. And care is funded by the government.

Contrast this with the US! Care is fragmented, costly, and complex to navigate. There are few resources to help find solutions. Caregiving in the US requires a lot more family or individual problem-solving, personal funding, assembling one's own resources, and integrating across healthcare providers and settings of care. Add to this the complexity of legal and practical differences state by state and a large country with vast distances between family members, and caregiving takes on a whole new level of challenge. It becomes its own job.

For me, every trip home to Malaysia meant encountering the dreaded questions from well-meaning neighbors and friends: "Can't you take your parents with you to look after them?" "Why don't you come live here with them when they need you?" "How are they living on their own here even though they have three children? Poor things, we pity them." It went on and on, innocent but devastating questions.

The answers to these questions were always complicated, imperfect, unsatisfying. I needed to earn a salary to pay for their care. I did not have residency or citizenship in Malaysia, so I couldn't work there. They chose not to move to the US when we asked them and it was still possible; it was too late later. These are diaspora issues that people cannot understand unless they have experienced them. When you move countries, you are limited by what set of rights and freedoms you have to live and work in a given place. We don't always think of these limitations before they become a crisis—when it is often too late to make changes. Even living in a different state or city from your parents comes with challenges, as many laws and regulations are different in each state and can be challenging when dealing with medical, legal, and financial decisions. So bear this in mind if your parents are not living close to you, and begin to think about how you may have constraints during caregiving that you need to anticipate and be aware of in a proactive manner.

My family certainly didn't think through the implications of all this in the earlier years when things were fine and good. A big one was my lack of citizenship and status in Malaysia. I could not sign on as an additional member of my parents' bank accounts—and we are still trying to figure out how to access their funds. The Islamic bank where they had some savings only allows sons to take the money out, as sons get preference in inheritance according to sharia laws. There are so many sociopolitical challenges we had been unaware of entirely. It took all our problem-solving skills to navigate those last years, along with the help of friends and healthcare professionals and kind strangers.

Being a caregiver from a distance is tricky, and when that distance is halfway across the planet and separated by a twelve-hour time zone difference, it gets even more challenging. Banking, getting nursing and medical resources, monitoring care, ensuring safety, and providing emotional and practical support are all extra tough when it takes over twenty hours in a plane to get to them in person. But there is always a silver lining to things. For us, the cost of care was much lower than in the US, and that provided greater flexibility.

So it is important to take stock early on in the journey of available resources close to your parents and have a range of options so that when the need is intensive, you are not starting from scratch. Use of tech is also important, which means making the tech accessible to parents and caregivers. We had all kinds of devices but not a practical approach to using them for the particular situation. Language, skills, willingness, and ability of each person to use the tech needs to be considered.

Being cognizant of these different perspectives and situations is important in thinking about the caregiving journey. Again, planning and dialogue become important so that we don't make the wrong assumptions, and so that we make decisions that respect and value the impact on everyone closely involved in the journey.

Because of cultural, generational, and individual differences, it is important to talk about your wishes and to explain your *why*—the rationale for why you feel how you feel about caregiving. This can help create a shared understanding and buy-in because, chances are, you will be leaning heavily on your partner, siblings, or other involved parties. So if they come with a different set of expectations, you will need to build mutual understanding and acceptance. Don't assume that anyone has the same ideas around caregiving; first open up discussions so that you can establish a baseline of expectations and then work to align on how you will solve for the needs you have in your responsibility.

I have lived in the US since I was eighteen, far from all my extended family as well as my parents. So it wasn't until later trips to Malaysia that I would see how elderly parents were so present in many homes. They were not necessarily perfectly cared for by each family, but they were not "abandoned" to nursing homes, which barely existed and were seen as a dumping ground for parents who had unfilial children. What was interesting was to see how older parents were integrated into daily life and coexisted with children and grandchildren. It was moving to see the diligence of family members who provided for the elderly and included them in everyday activities. They were given security and comfort and the most important thing—not being alone.

In the US, however, I found that many older people much preferred to live on their own as long as they could because they valued their independence and not being beholden to the schedules and meals and expectations of anyone else. What seems ideal and preferred in one culture or country can be the exact opposite in another. This is also the case on an individual basis: What may be ideal for one person can be a nightmare for another.

So keep in mind when making your own caregiving plan and executing it that you should be aware and respectful of the choices of your parents, partners, siblings, and everyone on your care team. Seek to build understanding and alignment on what path you will choose and be open to perspectives other than your own.

PART THREE

*Facing the Inevitable
and Moving Forward*

7

Approaching the Final Destination

At some point in the caregiving journey there is often a distinct change in outlook. Earlier you may see your loved one decline gradually, continuing at a somewhat steady state, sometimes punctuated by hospital stays or major procedures. That can feel like a roller coaster and have you wondering, *How long does this stage last? Will they get better or worse next?* All this can be quite confusing and exhausting. But then comes a moment when the end is clear and unavoidable. Things shift emotionally when you move from trying to keep your parent alive to ensuring that their end is as peaceful and painless as can be. There are many variations during this stage of the journey: Sometimes death comes quickly, while other times the end is seemingly near but choices have to be made about how that happens.

For the caregiver, it can be traumatic because you are

saying goodbye to a parent and giving up the push that you have been making to take care of them. As the situation changes, so does your approach to caregiving. It is a time to reconcile any issues that are lingering and cannot be delayed any further. Communications with family and friends become urgent, as you want to give every important person a chance to show up or connect so they are not left feeling out of the loop and with regrets. For the parent you are caring for, it may be a time of fear, pain, confusion, or loneliness, so do whatever you can to make their passing wholesome. And if you are emotionally falling apart, it can be the most important time to lean on your supporters.

Losing a parent is a painful experience, and there is no playbook. No way to train for it. You just have to experience it, and it can be profound. Along with the emotional magnitude of a parent's passing comes the logistical work that needs to be taken care of: final medical decisions, funeral arrangements, the funeral and burial or memorial service, and the managing of all the immediate business around property, assets, support team, pets, and so on. It's a tsunami of activity that can quickly overwhelm.

Preparations for some of this work can be made in advance, easing the immediate burden at time of death. But perhaps the most important thing is to be aware of this inevitable stage of caregiving. This means being ready to support your parent to the very end and creating an atmosphere of love, acceptance, and peace for everyone who is involved. Everyone dies. It is the cycle of the human experience and a reality for caregivers. And it is a gift you give your loved one when you provide them the best possible ending.

This chapter will go over both the logistics that need to be considered for end-of-life care as well as the emotional side of things. Letting go is incredibly difficult, so if you can approach the end knowing you have done your best to support your loved one, then you will be able to look back without guilt and regrets, and eventually you will be able to put some perspective on that last stage of caregiving. Here are some specifics we'll discuss:

- Understand what it means to take your loved one to the hospital or call an ambulance for them.
- If your loved one is on Medicare or other programs, understand the different kinds of hospital admission and what is covered.
- Understand what a Physician Orders for Life-Sustaining Treatment (POLST) form is and make sure you know how to get one.
- Get familiar with hospice and palliative care options in your community and what it means to use them.

LOGISTICS OF END-OF-LIFE CARE

As you approach this caregiving destination, there are resources and professionals available to help. While these are helpful, it is up to you to be as knowledgeable as possible about the process and how the system works. While we are not physicians and don't offer medical advice, as caregivers, knowing more about end-of-life possibilities and processes would have been beneficial.

When you are caregiving for a person with any cognitive or long-term issues, you need to be very clear about when to call an ambulance to take them to a hospital and when not to. If you are working with hospice, they can advise you, but it is your decision. You must consider each situation and understand what the wishes are of your loved one regarding care. Is it a life-threatening situation? Is an ambulance with trained paramedics required? What about your loved one's dignity? This is why understanding their wishes before they reach a state of decline is critical. Shari's dad did not want to be in a hospital, and at ninety-four, what a hospital could offer him was limited. They relied on the council of hospice so that he could stay where he was comfortable.

If you are caregiving for someone on Medicare, make sure you understand what the different kinds of hospital admittance mean and what is covered. For example, a patient can physically be in the hospital but just be considered under observation, which means they are not admitted as an inpatient. They're in a hospital bed, getting tests and treatments, and being monitored, but doctors are still deciding if they need to be formally admitted. Even though it feels like a hospital stay, Medicare sees this as outpatient care, not inpatient. This is important because it affects how Medicare pays (Part B instead of Part A), what you pay out of pocket, and whether the patient is eligible for skilled nursing care afterward (observation days don't count toward the three-day inpatient rule).

If they are admitted, be sure you understand how to get them discharged and get a POLST form. This is critical if caregiving for people who are older and frail or have chronic or advanced illness.

Hospice and palliative care are excellent options, both of which can be offered at home and in assisted living, or for hospice only in a hospice facility. The scope of services they offer is slightly different depending on the need. For example, hospice is comfort care at the end of life and hospice nurses are extremely knowledgeable, helping you prepare and take appropriate steps to make sure your loved one is comfortable. They can also help you navigate healthcare situations that in most cases aren't well structured for the aging, terminally ill, or those with dementia and Alzheimer's. They know what it means to call an ambulance when you are caregiving and they help you understand this.

Palliative care is comfort care that can occur at any time. It offers a range of services for improving the quality of life for someone facing a serious illness. Similar to hospice, palliative care serves the physical, emotional, and spiritual needs of both the patient and their family. Some examples of care would be symptom management, care coordination, advanced planning, counseling, and transition of care, to name a few. The biggest factor in choosing between these care options is the stage of the one you are caregiving for. Local resources can be found through a health provider, hospital, assisted living facility, or the internet.

WHEN THE END COMES BEFORE LIFE IS OVER

There is a point in all our journeys when we have to accept that time does not have a rewind button. We all get one chance to make the most of it. When you are caregiving, there is a critical moment when you acknowledge the forward momentum and realize nothing is going to stop life from flowing in that direction. Another aspect of this moment is when it seems your loved one has stopped living before they die. This might look like the sparkle leaving their eyes or a sense that while they are physically with you, they are not really the same person. As you get closer to the end with dementia patients, the moments of clarity and conversation become fewer and far between. You cherish those moments when they recognize you, greet you with a smile, or say your name.

This is one of the hardest parts of caregiving. As the end approaches, oftentimes your loved one may go into a state where they are still breathing but no longer talking, eating, or opening their eyes. This is the time to reflect, be present, and honor them. I fundamentally believe that in many of these cases, your loved one knows when the time is right. I have heard stories of families holding vigils at the bedside of their dying parent only to step out momentarily—and that is the moment their loved one passes. In other cases, the whole family is present when the last breath is taken. Dementia and Alzheimer's patients can sometimes forget how to swallow, so they will stop eating and drinking. While painful for us to witness, this state of the end arriving before life is over can be common and oftentimes starts an additional grieving process.

Shabnam

The nature of the end-of-life years has changed with all the improvements in medicine, but we haven't figured out how to make the extended physical years easier. My mother's parents both died in their sixties from heart attacks, while my mother lived to eighty-six with the help of good cardiovascular interventions and drugs but with dementia in the last few years—and we haven't figured out how to deal with dementia and Alzheimer's, have we? Are the extra years really worth it if someone doesn't even recognize their children and has none of their cognition, personality, or true self left?

For caregivers, there are many questions on how to care for parents with issues that can extend for years and years. I grieved my mother for two years even when she was still alive. There was a deep sense of loss that I could not fully accept because my mother was alive, but I was angry, sad, and upset—even embarrassed—at how she looked and that she was a lesser self without her true spirit and personality. I would cry at missing my mother, but then feel terrible because how could I grieve someone who was still alive? And I hated thinking about her just existing. *What is the point,* I would think to myself. *What sort of life is this when she cannot be the amazing force and influence that she has been all her life?*

The absence of that person made me angry about the existence of the person who was now in her place. But she was still my dear beloved mother, and I struggled to reconcile all these mixed feelings. Dementia is a terrible disease because it changes the person you love and you can never get them back, but the person they become each day is someone strange and aloof, unable to even recognize the care and love you are giving. Caregiving becomes a less gratifying experience and a true labor of love.

She wasn't the mother I wanted and needed, but she was

still my mother. I wanted her to have every care and comfort I could provide—so that was how I approached it, clinically, practically. I dreaded calling home to check in. I wanted the mother I loved and admired and who was a friend and adviser. We used to talk for hours about things happening at my work and brainstorm ways to handle people and situations. She was masterful at managing people and building relationships and figuring out how to get things done. We would joke and gossip and plan outings and share stories. But with dementia, she was like a happy infant: delighted at getting sweets and blandly sitting, looking at nothing, unable to understand global news or the goings-on in my life.

It was horrible to see that I had lost my true mother, who had always been my advocate and the person whom I could go to for the ultimate security and safety. All that was gone. I would no longer have the safety net I had relied on all my life. She would have hated to see herself like this—no longer the decision maker, she was like a child, amused by simple things and dependent on others for everything. She was dressed in simple clothes that were practical for caregivers but would be complete anathema to her sophisticated, fashionable earlier self.

One day, when I called home, my mother was really happy. She said one of the helpers had gifted her a bird, and the bird sang beautifully. I was so pleased to hear the joy in her voice. Mum had always gathered birds in our different homes, feeding them rice and bread and gradually building up a pattern where a group of birds would swoop in, have their goodies, and leave in a flurry. We enjoyed these visitors and Mum loved feeding them. But when I next went to visit my mother, I was shaken to the core. I realized the bird was a toy bird in a plastic cage and it "sang" whenever someone got close to it. In horror I realized that, to my dear mother in her state of dementia, the bird was real. It made me so incredibly sad and shocked to realize my mother's new reality. How could this be?! I wanted to run away from this whole phase of having a mother who was no longer her full self. That moment with the bird nearly killed me.

But I regrouped and realized the silver lining was that my mother was happy and the bird gave her joy. It did not matter that the bird was artificial. In caregiving, we have to meet people where they are and design moments for their happiness, not ours. The bird being a toy did not trouble anyone and it gave my mother joy. We followed up with a toy cat that purred and wagged its tail and also became her pet.

There is always something to be grateful for. She recognized me until almost the very end, and that was something. When I called and visited, I could see that she was healthy and well looked after in every way possible, and that was something too.

The first time I was on video with her and she did not know who I was really crushed me. It was the last time we spoke, as she passed away a couple of days later. I wonder if it was a sign to me that it was time to let go. I tell my children now that the day I don't recognize them is the last day I want to be alive. For me, there is no point in living that way; losing touch with your most precious ones is a clear reason to be done. As humans begin living even longer lives, we will need to have more frank conversations around choices about death, especially in situations where the person is in excruciating pain or no longer able to maintain their sense of self and awareness.

Alzheimer's and dementia are so hard for the people around the patient, and I wish I had had more understanding going into it. Even though I had read a lot about the illness online, I know I would have benefited from peer groups to understand the emotional impact of caregiving, and I encourage you to seek out this kind of support.

THINGS WILL CHANGE

Shari

There are many things you begin to realize in life as you grow older and wiser. Here are the ones that often bubble to the top for me: Life is incredibly beautiful if you can wake yourself up to see it, and the only real certainty in life is death. I do not mean that in a morbid, gloom-and-doom way but just realistically. While we can be confronted with death in a variety of ways throughout our lives, it is one thing we know without fail will happen to us. Some say accepting that death is your fate at some point makes you live more fully. Whether we choose to embrace death or not, mindset alone cannot ease the grief that accompanies loss.

It was a rainy November day in 2021, the kind you get a lot in the Pacific Northwest that time of year, where it is cold and gray—the perfect day to snuggle up inside. The world was slowly moving toward a new normal. I was attending a virtual executive retreat where we spent a productive two days reshaping the mission, vision, and company values. We had about two hours left in the retreat when I got a call from my father's retirement community.

I muted myself and shut my camera off to pick it up. The nurse informed me that they had found my dad lying on the floor with his head wedged between his bed and nightstand. They had sent someone to check on him when he failed to show up for breakfast and were uncertain how long he'd been like that.

I saw my father daily, as he lived just down the road from us. When I wasn't with him, he would call my sister, brother, kids, and me several times a day. We programmed all our numbers into his phone, and he would go through them to connect with everyone. Sometimes if there was an event at his assisted living home in the morning, he would call after. I had gotten so sucked into the retreat, I hadn't even realized my father had not called.

This wasn't the first time my dad had fallen recently, but this time felt different and the urgency in the voice of the nurse concerned me even more. Having just celebrated his ninety-fourth birthday, he was by all accounts a medical marvel.

I let my boss know I had to go and hopped in the car, bound for my dad's assisted living facility. When I arrived at his room, he was barely dressed and looked disheveled and extremely tired. As usual, when I walked in, he was so happy to see me and tried his best to mask the situation by asking me if I had eaten. I let him know we needed to go to the hospital, to get checked out after his fall. Despite the bruising on his arms and cuts on his head, my dad didn't remember the fall; he was in mid- to late-stage dementia. He did not want to go to the hospital, but since I asked him, he agreed, and we headed over to urgent care.

My dad and I had always been close, and I was now his caregiver as well as his daughter. And I had the utmost respect for him as a father and as a human. He had a power about him, a quiet confidence that drew people to him. He'd also had a full head of white hair for as long as I could remember. My last two years of high school were spent living just with my dad while my mother was in the hospital five hours away in Minnesota, waiting, receiving, and then completing the aftercare for her heart transplant. As a child I thought so differently than my father because he was the patriarch, the true rock of the family, but for him it was different. My mother was his rock, and when she passed away in 1999, he was never the same. I suspect she knew this could happen, as she'd always told me to make sure to take care of my dad.

Since he was a World War II veteran, our first stop was the Naval Hospital Urgent Care. They took one look at my dad and sent us to the local hospital. Covid was on another surge and the hospital was at full capacity, so we waited in the emergency room for sixteen hours, which is very difficult with a dementia patient who would rather be anywhere than at the hospital. We talked as my dad drifted in and out of sleep. As the hours wore on, the years rolled back for my dad. At one point he thought I was my mom, then his mom, and then finally his beloved older sister, Donna. She and my dad were close in age and spent a great deal of time together trying not to get tangled up with their Irish father, who loved the drink more than he did his own family.

We talked and sang (a godsend for us), he slept, and I planned. Every once in a while, he would wake up and not understand where he was or sometimes it seemed as though he was in a dream. At one point he was very upset he was going to be in trouble. "Who are you in trouble with?" I asked.

"The Church," he responded. "Surely the priest would be upset that this is not a Catholic hospital."

I assured him that was not the case and told him the hospital was named after the patron saint Michael, the champion of justice, a healer of the sick, and the guardian of the Church. "You are covered from the Catholic side of things, Dad," I said. As dementia works through a person, it is interesting to see the areas it hits and what remains. My dad never lost his faith; it was always deeply rooted in him. But this terrible disease had taken my beloved dad from me, the dad I remembered with kind eyes and a gracious heart. My parents always made me feel like I could do anything, and I spent a lot of time talking with them both. My dad always had the best and most insightful advice for all situations. He had a magic ability to snap back into reality when I needed it most. But that was not the dad I was with now.

During our time waiting for a doctor, we finally moved out of a bed in the hallway into a temporary room. My mind was constantly working: *How am I going to tell my work? How am I going to manage my dad through this?*

He was finally admitted to the hospital, but due to the Covid protocols, they would not let me stay overnight. So they assigned a full-time aide to my dad and had to secure him to the bed. He was not harmful to anyone but was confused, and if the circumstance had allowed, I believe he would have made a run for it—with or without his wing tip shoes. Hospitals are not great places for the aging, and they are especially difficult for patients with cognitive issues like dementia. With the noises and constant wake-ups, they are just completely overwhelmed.

When I saw my dad next, he could barely walk, his speech was slurred, and his cognitive decline was profound. I found out they were giving him a heavy dose of antipsychotic meds, which were the culprit for all the above. He had taken lisinopril for years for high blood pressure, but nothing else. So one could imagine the impact these high-powered meds had on him. They finally confirmed there was a cardiac incident, but what they can do for someone in their mid-nineties is limited.

When I finally caught the doctor, I had a candid conversation with him about the prognosis for my father. He told me that at this point, the only way he could release him would be to a one-to-one care setting. This meant he needed to go to a memory care or skilled nursing facility. I knew there was a memory care option on the grounds of his retirement community, so we started making calls. My sister confirmed they had a bed for him and could accept him anytime. The next morning, I started the process to get my dad released. He couldn't stay in the hospital any longer, and one of his desires was to not die in a hospital.

We were approaching day four and my sister was arriving the next day to help, as I was completely overwhelmed. I was managing, but barely. I knew I had to get to the hospital as soon as they started visiting hours to catch the doctor. Dad was sitting up and ready to go home when I arrived. I helped him comb his hair, shave, put on a clean shirt, and eat breakfast. After his fall, some days he could eat by himself and others he could not. Today was the latter and he did not have much of an appetite. He was sad and wanted to go back to his apartment and friends. When the doctor arrived, he said they would prepare my father for release that morning. I called to make sure the bed was ready at the memory care facility and got his clothes ready, and we waited. And waited. Nothing happened.

I checked in with the aide, who did not know the status, and then the social worker, and by 11:00 a.m. one of the nurses informed me it was very unlikely he would be released today, as I had missed the window. What window? Confused, I went to one of the caseworkers who helped me understand the process. The healthcare workers, the doctor, and my dad's team were truly amazing, caring, thoughtful, and candid. I could not have gotten through it without them. They saw hundreds of patients and knew that my dad did not belong in a hospital. They helped us get in touch with hospice and palliative care and investigate which option would be the right one for my dad.

The next morning, I arrived at the hospital, ready for my quest of discharge. I was fully informed on the process for release and waited for the doctor, who told me what I was missing yesterday was a POLST form with a diagnosis and care plan. He completed it, showed it to me, and said it needed a few additional signatures by a particular time or the release would not happen. I could not walk the form around, so I followed it from person to person. The aide got my dad ready, showered, and dressed to be discharged while I kept a close eye on the clock. My sister had arrived and then headed to the memory care facility to make sure everything there was ready to go.

After we got the signatures needed and ordered transport,

we were ready. We took my dad back to his assisted living community. This new unit was locked, meaning the residents could not go outside unless they were in a protected courtyard. He would not have the comforts of his apartment either. My dad was unable to stand, so he used a wheelchair. Entering this new space, I realized everything was going to be different. The life we had built with my dad and the fun we'd had with him was all about to change. I grieved for my kids, who loved their time with Papa Joe.

This is one of those situations where having someone around with experience would have been helpful. I later learned that we could have gotten my dad released to his existing apartment, just with a full-time caregiver present. There are so many questions we did not ask, because we did not know to ask them. Whatever your situation, be sure you make the situation work for you and your loved one. It may take some extra planning, but you can do it. We were driven to get my dad out of the hospital, but we did not spend enough time exploring options. At the time, the stress level was so high, it is not surprising we were not thinking clearly.

Just know as you move through these steps that there are options. For years, when I met with various healthcare providers or the team at the retirement community, they would say to be ready when an incident, a lot of times a fall, occurs. After that, the decline can happen rapidly. This fall was that life-changing moment for my dad.

CHAPTER TAKEAWAYS

Caregiving is such a meandering path, but when it enters the final stretch before the end of life, caregivers need to have heightened awareness and an action plan. Coming to terms with this stage is itself important so you can prepare both emotionally and logistically. Taking care of yourself in particular and allowing yourself to lean on others for help is so important. Supportive members of your care team can be a huge resource, and having plans in place so that you are not alone in managing this critical time is important. Anticipate that you will be stretched, know your options, and have communication channels ready so that you are proactive in reaching out to family members. If you can recognize that your parent has reached the last stage of their life and death is approaching rapidly, you will be better able to manage all the range of medical, family, and self-care needs that arise.

8

The Moment of Death

Just as there is a last stage of the caregiving journey in approaching the end of life for your loved one, there is a precise moment when life does, in fact, end. The time of passing can arrive in all sorts of settings and is a profound moment for you and everyone else who is close to your loved one. There is a shock to the soul when a human life that has mattered so much for as long as you can remember is no longer present. The role a parent plays is huge in your emotional development and so many facets of your life. Even when relationships are complicated or the experience is fraught with challenges, the loss of that life is of a magnitude that is hard to explain.

The majority of us will experience the death of a parent. We see it portrayed in movies, we might see our parents experience the loss of their own parents, we see spouses or friends lose their parents. But nothing can fully prepare you for the loss of your own parent. If you are there, present with them, and can witness a peaceful passing with your parent surrounded by loved ones, that may be the least painful way. Hearing about it when you are far away or not expecting it can be shocking and very sad. Choosing to not be present for whatever reason can have its own emotional baggage. Sometimes we choose and other times we have no control over the setting and atmosphere of the passing. Regardless, it is a moment that has meaning and impact that we need to experience and come to terms with in the long run.

Shabnam

We don't get to choose the nature or circumstances of the moment of death for our loved ones or ourselves, but we can reconcile with it, forgive ourselves for the imperfections, and be kind to ourselves in order to move on with grace.

My mother's reality in her state of dementia turned out to be a blessing at her moment of death. I had not been able to visit her for ten months as the border was closed during the height of the pandemic. It was heartbreaking to hear of my mother's loneliness and not have her understand why I could not come. It breaks my heart to this day because she thought we didn't care. Sometimes we have to just accept when there is nothing more we could have done and let go of the guilt.

I received a phone call from her helpers that they were taking her to the hospital. She had been unwell and sweating all night. At the hospital, it became clear she had been having a heart attack and would not live long. I was halfway across the world. It was so distressing to have to manage through the phone and know that I would not see her in person again, ever. It all happened in a blur and I was a mess. I had to manage somehow and attend her funeral through the phone, letting the people near her take care of everything. I did not have any closure and still find it painful to talk about.

However, now after some time and healing, I am able to hear the story of her moment of passing and even be amused, knowing that my mother went as she had always been, in control and bossing everyone to entertain her guests and make them feel welcome. In the hospital room, when my sisters-in-law and the helpers gathered to say goodbye, she thought she was in her own home and that guests had arrived. "Pushpa, bring some tea and biscuits for our guests," she said. How brilliant!

She was happy, felt she was doing her thing as a good host, and was completely unaware of being in a hospital about to die. How blessed—even though she had no immediate family with her, she was surrounded by loving people and without pain or fear. Only now can I look upon this silver lining and think what a perfect end for her.

My father's passing was even more traumatic for me than my mother's. He was on a feeding tube from his late-stage Parkinson's and bedridden, still being cared for with full-time care at home. But he kept pulling out his feeding tube. This was our sign that he wanted to be allowed to go, only we couldn't bring ourselves to see that happen. In hindsight, I should have listened better and respected his wish. One of my biggest regrets is not being able to let him go.

At the time, I had only thought of being the dutiful

daughter doing the heroic work and keeping her father alive at all cost. But I was doing that for me, not for him. Little did I know that was so unfair to him! He could not eat except through a tube in his nose. Perhaps nature has its own way of telling us when life is not sustainable. My father never, ever complained, but he did ask to be let go. I urge you to keep this in mind during your own journey: Think about your actions and how they will affect your loved one.

My father also ended up in the wrong hospital—not the fancy private hospital where I had enabled all his care but the nearby government hospital that was full of good doctors but only the most basic care. It was a place that took patients in who had nowhere to go and no money to pay. That was a most traumatic experience for me because my father was in an open ward with patients suffering all around him. I cannot even write about what I saw as I sat with him for days. It is too painful to talk about, still.

The doctors begged us to let my father go. He could not speak or eat, could barely breathe on his own. They wanted all three children to sign off, but my brothers were in California and Australia in different time zones and hard to reach. Even when they had agreed, it was up to me as the only one who was there in person to give the final okay. That ripped my heart to shreds. I knew it had to be done, but I had never done anything so difficult as to say, *Yes, go ahead and let my father die.*

I held his hand until he was gone. Now, I miss that last feeling of touching him, of letting go, of knowing I would never have his love again. It was such a precious love that I did not think it possible to want to live without it. No day since or ahead can be as good as it could have been with him alive and present in my life. That is the price of love: living with its absence.

Shari

After my dad's fall, life was a series of ups and downs. He was dropped from hospice because he was gaining weight, but then it was clear he needed that care. I met with the input person on Sunday, ordered everything we needed, and the nurse was coming by the next day for an exam and to meet with my dad. It was the same nurse we'd had before, which was great. She was supposed to arrive in the afternoon but instead came in the morning, so I missed her. She called me after and said my dad had dramatically declined since she'd last seen him, about a month ago. She was not a fan of us getting him up every day and moving him around the facility and thought we needed to focus more on his comfort.

By this time, I was going over multiple times a day to help him get up, dress him, comb his hair, and do the tasks he liked done daily. My dad used a wheelchair and needed assistance eating, drinking, going to the bathroom, and getting around. Some days he would talk, but other days he would not. I was making food at home for him and bringing it over so at least he could have something he liked when he did eat, which was not often. He did like cake, though I had to blend it up because he couldn't understand how to use his dentures any longer and I was afraid he would choke on them. I also made him a Spotify playlist with a bunch of his favorite music so I could try to calm him.

My heart and body were heavy with grief. Some days I could see that sparkle in his eyes, but it was brief. Many days we would sit in silence. Oftentimes he would mistake me for my mom, his sister, or his mother. I wondered where his mind was, and the weight of knowing I was not going to get him back was paralyzing at times. Dementia is a cruel disease. It takes your loved one from you slowly and painfully. Despite all of this, there were times I could really see him, and if I held his hand, he might squeeze mine back. I took this as a sign he was still there, just less than he had been before.

As the days progressed, his agitation grew and he was difficult to move. I had to rely on the staff, who used a lift to get him in and out of bed or to the bathroom. I did what I could to make him comfortable, telling him how much we loved him and that it was okay for him to go and be with my mom. I had a board meeting coming up in New York and asked the hospice nurse whether I should go. She told me she thought it was fine, that his condition probably would not change in the few days I'd be gone. But then, the night before I left, my dad started to breathe very differently. I called the nurse, who was planning on visiting him the next day. I spent the evening with him and hopped a red-eye to New York. I did not sleep much and headed into the office. I stepped away from my desk, and when I returned, I had missed a call from the nurse.

When I called her back, she told me that my dad was actively dying and that I needed to come back immediately. "Is there anyone who can come be with your father?" she asked. I called my husband, who jumped in the car and spent the day with my dad. I don't really remember this day, but I do know I had an incredible group of coworkers who helped me find a flight and get back home. My boss's assistant walked with me back to my hotel to help me pack. While I was there, my husband got us all (my siblings, kids, nieces, and nephews) on a FaceTime call and we each said goodbye to my dad. We were all crying and it was an out-of-body experience. *This can't be happening,* I thought. I was completely numb.

I got in a car and made it to the airport for my flight. I was texting back and forth with my husband until I didn't have service. Finally, after five hours, we landed at Sea-Tac and I let my husband know I would be there in forty minutes. He told my dad I had landed and would be there soon. He then said my dad partially sat up, took a big breath, and lay back down. Then he was gone.

I could not believe it. I remember walking through the airport to my car and all I could hear was a loud noise, a deafening noise of no sound. When I arrived at the facility, my husband was in the room with my dad and I immediately opened the windows, an Irish tradition to let the spirit leave. We called hospice and sat with my dad, waiting for their arrival. I struggled with this moment and my choice to leave, but then I realized this is how my dad wanted it to be. He did not want us to be with him when he passed. He was our caretaker, and he felt very comfortable with my husband and knew he would take care of me.

The hospice nurses arrived and did their checks and called the time of death. They then informed us we needed to call the funeral home. We hadn't done any of the funeral preparations in advance, but the staff at our funeral home were very helpful and it was past midnight when they finally arrived. They were extremely professional, and when it was time, politely asked us to step out of the room. I had no idea how hard this moment would be.

I completely broke down as the reality of the situation stormed down on me. I was never going to see my dad, my amazing dad, and his kind face again. I was not going to hear his voice, hold his hand, or hug him. It was the most awful and painful feeling. When they were ready, we walked down the corridor with them, and when I looked up, I saw my dad and my mom at the end of the hall. They were holding hands and smiling at me, a pose I had seen so many times in my life. I knew this was what my dad had dreamed about for so many years, being back with my mom. It was hard to think that these two people who meant so much to me would now both live forever in my memories and in all of us who'd had a chance to experience them.

Despite having gone through this with my mom years before, no amount of preparation can help you when the moment of death actually arrives. It is one of the heaviest moments I know. For my mom's passing, it was something we had been expecting and a celebration of the years we'd had with her. For my dad's, it was peaceful but finite. I believe that when a person passes away, their body leaves but their spirit lives on in all of us. Even still, losing the physical presence and facing the reality of both your parents being gone is truly a painful experience.

It is hard to grieve then because the moment they pass away, you have to immediately kick into managing the business of death.

THE BUSINESS OF DEATH

After loss has occurred, the business of death kicks in—and it is a process. If you are unprepared for it, there are so many decisions and payments to make that you barely have time to grieve. The business of death includes choosing a funeral home; deciding on burial versus cremation, or other options; looking at urns, coffins, headstones, flowers, invitations, churches, and other details; finding the right date and time for services; and more. Given the gravity of the situation, these details can feel trivial. If you are able, the best thing to do is discuss these tasks with your loved one in advance so you not only can have the details squared away but also will know you're doing things exactly as they wanted. Depending on your culture, these decisions and processes can vary dramatically.

If you were able to take the proper steps with the estate, this is when you will feel the benefits of this prework. If you are using a funeral home, it's advantageous to have one preselected so it is easy to get in touch with them upon loss. They start their process, which includes picking up your loved one when you are ready. When it comes to funeral services, many funeral homes give you the option to have a funeral director. The benefit of a funeral director is they have a templated process that is almost plug-and-play. It can be a relief to not have to make every decision. Other decisions important to have in advance are burial or cremation, as this dictates whether you need a casket and location for burial or an urn. Or there are more eco-friendly modern options such as green funerals or human composting.

A piece of advice that hospice gave us was to get multiple

copies of the death certificate. You will need them. If you are moving your loved one's remains across states, you will need this plus either a certificate or permission to carry cremains or transport a body on an airline. The interesting thing is that everything is very clear and, in most cases, there is one specific process to follow. It is a contrast to the process of caregiving, where often there is a wealth of information but no specifics.

Shari

We had my dad's celebration of life on Memorial Day. My dad's wish was to be buried in South Dakota next to my mom. We did all the scheduling and set up for the funeral remotely, opting not to have a funeral director. This meant that I was the de facto funeral director on top of many other roles, so my siblings and I divided and conquered the planning. Luckily, the small town I grew up in is full of families who knew my father, and so many of them stepped up to help us plan a proper celebration. As a lifelong Irish Catholic, my dad loved the church, and that was the only thing he knew as far as religion went. We thought it was best that we have a funeral mass back in our parish in South Dakota. It was a beautiful service with so many relatives present, along with a fair amount of grief and sadness when we finally left my father alongside my mother.

The blessing in all of this is that the business component makes this mostly transactional. And if you have the opportunity to plan in advance, it is very much about showing up. This can make the whole process easier. The hardest part begins after the business is completed. At that point, you may be hit with a rush of emotions to process. Just be prepared for the emotions to be overwhelming at times.

DEATH RITUALS

Shabnam

My mother-in-law passed away in Malaysia on December 23, 2024. It was not a surprise, she did not suffer, and she had four of her five children with her as well as a granddaughter and a great-granddaughter. But it was still a shock to the family and it did make me wonder: *What is it about the year-end holidays in that they are often a time for death and loss?*

It is an interval when working adults tend to have time off, which means they can congregate with their extended families. And maybe that is the reason—what better time to pass on than when surrounded by your loved ones? One may wonder if there really is any control to when we let go, and yet somehow I feel there is more connection between mind and body than we understand.

My mother-in-law had been fading since about two years prior. Even though she was mobile, positive, and relatively happy, it felt like she was at peace with all she had accomplished, and she was becoming less of a force in the house. Older people become invisible in some ways, left out of decision-making and socializing and not feeling important to the lives of their once-dependent children. Being needed is a strong human driver. My mother-in-law had her garden that gave her joy, her home that continues to serve her children and the next generations, and no pending obligations. She had lived a life of giving love, serving others, and being a huge force for good to everyone who came near her. A life well lived. But everyone goes at some point, and her children now have to reconcile with her passing and her absence.

At the end of the day, all religions attempt to do the same thing—provide a collective goodbye and a process to connect those who remain with the good memories of the departed, and offer solace and healing. Regardless of the specific processes and rituals, whether church or mosque or temple, there is comfort in knowing what to expect and guidance to help everyone come to terms with the passing. Even though we all die, it is so very difficult to deal with it and move on.

There are small mercies along the way sometimes. For my husband and his family, they knew they were all loved by their mother and she had no wants that were not covered. She was able to remain in her own home until the end as she had always wished. She lived until ninety-three and was cared for by multiple people in multiple ways. She was even able to greet a great-grandchild, and she was with her children right to the last breath. A best-case scenario. I would feel blessed to have such an end.

My husband had spent a lot of time in Malaysia with his mother two years before her death. Since he retired, he'd spent one to two months a couple of times a year there. He knew his mother would not live forever and those moments mattered. It is so fortunate he was able to do this because now there are no regrets and his conscience is clear. (That is a goal!)

A big takeaway is to not put off things that matter, because you can't know how much time you have. By showering love and care on his mother, and by being there a lot toward the end, my husband got to be present when she passed. In Asia, being in the presence of an elder who passes away is seen as a gift, an honor. I found it strange at first, but then when my father passed away, I understood—the moment is incredibly moving and special and deep. A transition, a goodbye, a mystery.

Rituals are interesting and important to think about as well. There is a relief in the fact that professionals take over, whether priests or imams or community elders. It takes the burden off the family to be guided through the farewell process. One feels comfort in that there are people who are tasked with following a process, and the community comes together in that process. There is often beauty in words through music, chants, and prayer, and people come to sit with you so you are not alone in dealing with the shock and grief. I remember the funeral of a neighbor who left behind two young children; it was so awful and tragic, but the funeral home was filled to capacity with her friends, colleagues, family, and mentees. It was clear that she had been of influence to so many. It was a reminder to everyone who showed up that we should each aspire to a life that touches others well.

After my mother-in-law's passing, many people came to the house to provide condolences and sit with the family. Even the contractor who had done work around the house came by and paid his respects. Each person's visit and kind words provided healing to the family. Another lesson—show up for people whenever you can; even if it seems a small thing to you, it could mean a lot to them. It is the best of humanity when we can share in difficult times and give a virtual or real hug to loved ones.

CHAPTER TAKEAWAYS

If you have the opportunity, put some planning and thought into the final moment for your parent. According to their wishes, arrange to have people present who matter and will be a comfort to you. Create a set of conditions that minimize the difficulties around facing a heartbreaking moment, as it is one that can leave you unable to think clearly. Lean on those who are close to you and able to provide emotional and logistical help, taking ownership of decisions that need to be made quickly. Most importantly, give yourself space to be fully present and keep yourself healthy so you can be strong in your own journey of grief and recovery.

Acknowledge the moment and lean on your faith, friends, and family. Allow yourself to turn the page on this important chapter of your life. We cannot predict exactly how and when this moment will appear in our lives, but we can be aware that it occurs and prepare to some degree so that we can look back on it someday with acceptance of an inevitable part of the human experience. As a caregiver, feeling you did the best you could for your parent can help to let go. Supporting them as they pass away can be a challenge and a blessing, so do what you can to be able to remember it with love and without guilt and regret.

9

Making Peace and Moving Forward

After a loved one we have been focused on caregiving for dies, we are often left feeling unclear about how to proceed. Caregiving becomes a part of our identity and that, along with our loved one, has been ripped away. With this moment comes a deep grief.

There are many resources available to help manage grief, and tools such as therapy and medications can be useful as well. But grief is a complicated thing and no one solution works for everyone. Recovering from grief is not a linear or straightforward process. It might be fairly brief for some and prolonged for others, in some cases even debilitating without professional help. What is important to know is that no one shapes your grief or recovery but you. All the people around you can support you if you give them guidance on how to do that, but sometimes you may not even know how to express what you need.

Grief won't hesitate to remind you that everyone and everything you love will disappear someday. The ones who carry grief typically love with a passion and fierceness that no one else understands because they know what it feels like to let someone go. So they start to remember the little things and they show up when it counts. They know that as beautiful and precious as love is, it comes with a cost, and they are willing to take it on without fear. Grief changes shape, but it doesn't end. The beauty of this is you can keep some of your loved one with you forever.

A friend who's also a social work counselor once told us, "When you lose a parent, there will be a hole in your heart; that hole will not go away, but in time you will learn to live around it." This was such a meaningful framework because it helped us understand and work through the recovery period.

In this chapter, we discuss how there is no clear timing on how to recover from grief, and yet you should be your own advocate and manager to get the help you need. Dedicate yourself to recovery so that you can return to a healthy and productive life, even though there will be poignant reminders that suddenly bring grief back. Learning to live through it and with it should be a priority in your post-caregiving life. You have done important work; now focus on reclaiming your health and well-being.

UNDERSTANDING GRIEF

Shari

Grief! I don't have a magical formula for recovering from grief, but I do know that taking time off work helped me begin to better understand how to process my grief. I am very grateful for the opportunity; it was life-changing. I had lots of stored grief that was affecting me and holding me back in a variety of ways, and I had to release it. Trauma is experienced differently by all of us because we are unique individuals. But a key way for anyone to release grief is to cry, one of the more challenging things for me to do. While I can cry during Tide commercials or even at the thought of my parents, I did not honor myself well in crying throughout the years. I had to be the strong one always.

When my mother died, I had to hold it together because my dad could not. I learned to process my grief in different, maybe not-so-productive ways. I buried it and distracted myself. What I discovered after my dad's death was that I armored up in tough circumstances and never processed my feelings. During my year off, I finally took the time to process and release my grief, which allowed me to rebuild a connection to myself. I focused on taking better care of myself, resting, eating well, exercising, and crying. I don't mind crying, but I don't love doing it in front of people, so I am working on building this skill. What I have learned is that water cleanses the body and tears cleanse the soul. So let it flow, my friends.

The five stages of grief are:

- **Denial:** Your mind won't let you accept reality, which can give you more time to process news gradually. This can numb you to your true feelings about the situation.
- **Anger:** This is usually directed at someone or something. Anger can hide true feelings and is often used as a defense mechanism so you don't feel your sadness.
- **Bargaining:** This is when you try to tell yourself you are okay, though it is common to feel often like you did not do enough. You may ask yourself "what if" questions, looking for a way to maintain control of the situation.
- **Depression:** This can be isolation, sadness, anxiety, or really just a loss of interest in doing anything. You may feel overwhelmed, confused, or spiritually or emotionally heavy.
- **Acceptance:** You accept the loss, pain, and all that goes with it.

There is no correct way to move through these steps. People typically skip around, starting and stopping, staying in one stage a long time, and sometimes skipping another. When I lost my mother, I did not really go through bargaining; I was parked at anger, then flipped to depression. My anger was at God: *Why my mom?* The thought of having to accept a reality, a world without my mom when I was in my late twenties was not one I wanted to face. It was my priest at the time, Father Jack, who really helped me through this process.

Besides these stages, there are also many different types

of grief, from anticipatory to collective grief. In 2021, I started having dreams about losing my dad. They were all different but typically involved scenarios with traditional Catholic funerals and wakes. When my dad fell and we had to release him to memory care, these dreams became more frequent. I was often called in the middle of the night if he had fallen out of bed, or I would wake up feeling like something happened and would go over to see if he was all right.

When my mother coded in about the twelfth year after her transplant, she was in the hospital in South Dakota and I lived in Chicago. It was the middle of the night and I shot out of bed at 3:00 a.m. with a jolt of energy I had never felt in my life; it was like I had been stabbed and was choking. I did not have any idea what was going on and thought I was just stressed, so I hopped on my bike and headed to the gym at 4:00 a.m., about a fifteen-minute bike ride from my house. By the time I arrived, my brother had called and told me Mom had coded. Though she had started breathing on her own again, I needed to get home to South Dakota immediately. I left the gym, grabbed a cab, and headed to O'Hare with only my backpack and work clothes.

This middle-of-the-night episode was how I experienced anticipatory grief. And cumulative grief, when you are working through multiple losses, is where I believe I am now. Grief can take from six months to over two years to process, though that is just a general timeline.

When you are caregiving and then lose your loved one, there can be so much compiled grief that bubbles up, and it is complicated by so many factors. When you start caregiving, it is almost impossible to spend time thinking about yourself.

There are still swim meets, lacrosse practices, and soccer matches on the weekend. There are still groceries that need to be bought and laundry that needs to get cleaned. There are still long days at the office and work crises to be dealt with. Suddenly, all the caregiving time was taken off my plate, and I didn't want the void to just be full of grief.

I decided I was going to fill that extra time with more work. While my heart ached, I jumped on a plane and started to work more. When I reflect on it now, I realize it was a way for me to mask the grief that I had and the pain of loss that was staring me right in the face.

I remember, one day, actually driving home and feeling physically and mentally exhausted. If you get to this point, your thoughts may not be healthy, but I kept going. I didn't have time to stop. What I didn't realize is that it wasn't just grief for the loss of my dad. I was dealing with the grief from becoming a caretaker. The grief that I had from losing him to dementia. The guilt and shame, especially from when he was really sick and having such a hard time and I didn't know how to help him. And I had never properly grieved the loss of my mother, so that was coming up too. I was on grief overload. There was no more room; I had to let this stored grief go.

I know I have just begun the process of working through some of my repressed grief. And as for everything, there is no handbook, checklist, or clean way of moving through it because we are all different. Acknowledging and understanding it is really a giant step in the right direction.

As the years pass, I still dream about my parents, but over time their roles in my dreams have changed. They typically don't speak but are just always present, now mostly in the back of the room, watching and smiling. This mimics how they exist in my subconscious—watchful, present, and forever supportive. I still tear up and smile at the same time when I think of my parents because I loved them and miss them so much.

I find myself having to pause for a moment to actually accept that they are gone. I am moving into coping with grief and acknowledging what that feels like for me, releasing the parts I want to and cherishing and honoring the parts I need to. It has been a very intense process for me, but if you give yourself this time and honor what you need, it will help you get to a better, more manageable place with your grief.

Shabnam

Grieving felt like being trapped in a fishbowl and looking out at people going about their lives, knowing they had no idea what was going on with me. I was trapped in it, barely able to function. The days after losing my dad and being back in New Jersey are a blur now after seven years, but I can still feel the pain. I could not get out of bed. Many, many days I lay curled up, unable to face the world. I was angry and upset and unwell. It felt like everyone who came to see me was saying things that should make me feel better but just didn't. "I am so sorry for your loss" is well meant, but it wasn't something I was open to receiving at that time.

One day a friend suggested we take a walk by the river in Princeton, so I went with her, but I got so angry and upset at her not having a clue about how I was feeling. *How could she really—she has her parents still*, I thought. I think I scared her with my intensity and anger. Some days I could not deal with seeing friends; other days I was angry that they were staying away. My husband and children were bewildered about what to do for me—and I didn't help because I was in that fishbowl and unable to figure out how to get out of it. Everyone felt remote, and I was alone. Sleep was disrupted with nightmares of all kinds and left me even more tired.

Several months went by and I slowly learned to pretend like I was okay because I wanted people to not worry. A friend who counsels families grieving from loss due to cancer gave me important advice: "Help people to help you by telling them what you want in any given moment. Grieving is normal, and there is no time limit. You will learn to live around the hole in your soul." This finally seemed to kick in and propel me forward.

Getting back to work in a start-up company (facilitated by my caring and wise mentor, Tim Rothwell) was a big part of my recovery. Finding a worthy mission and fantastic people to be around was great; these were all people who did not know me previously, so I could meet them fresh. They did not need to know about my situation, and I felt liberated from the grief and awkwardness that comes when people don't know how to talk to you about your loss. A new environment was so therapeutic, as it allowed me to shed the past pain and show up as a happy person focused on work. I could be fun, optimistic, and light in spirit whenever I was in that work environment. Perhaps a lesson here is that if you can change up your surroundings, it can release you for periods of time from the things that remind you of your loss.

But at the same time, I could not talk about my father

without diving back into grief. It was embarrassing because my eyes would well up with tears and my voice would choke. I immediately felt out of control and hysterical, and I'd wonder how long it would last. Would I ever be able to think of my father and speak of him without breaking down? Other people did not seem to have this level of messiness when they lost a parent. They seemed to cope so much better, and I felt like something was wrong with me.

I learned that often people hide their grief well, but a shared moment of understanding can create an instant bond. This is why it's important to not lock up your experiences. Knowing that you are not alone and that you are not crazy is so important in moving forward. Other people can help. Now I can almost talk about my parents without visible tears, though the pain is still palpable in my heart.

FINDING YOUR WAY

Shabnam

I woke up one day to a post on Facebook from a dear friend who had just lost her grandfather. It was a stunningly beautiful post about a man who had lived to ninety-two, and almost every photo showed him embracing someone—children, grandchildren, great-grandchildren, friends, and family. He had been the life of the party and adored by everyone around him. His loss was already deeply felt because of the love he had given and the big group of people who had surrounded him until the end. For my friend, even knowing that he was in his nineties and increasingly frail, his passing came as a shock.

It made me reflect on how we as humans struggle with facing the realities of old age—although maybe that is a survival mechanism and part of our humanity. We hang on to our loved ones in spite of the odds because we cannot imagine a world (our world) without them.

It is still a shock to me sometimes to realize my mother and father are no longer here. That takes a moment to process, the twinge of grief, of feeling this world is so much less than it could be because they are not here with me. I have a feeling of being less protected, less loved, less complete. Yes, it is inevitable that we all die, but it seems impossible to work with that on a day-to-day basis. Now that I've been through it, I see my friends who are caregiving for their parents experiencing the dread of loss and the denial of its possibility.

Looking back, I realize I had not seen many aging people in their final stages before caregiving for my parents, and I wonder if that experience would have better prepared me for my own journey. In the US, we live more modular lives, and it is not often that multiple generations live together (a trend that is becoming more common in many parts of the world). When I see families living in proximity with their elders, there is a more comfortable approach to accepting aging and passing; it is a natural process and less of an overwhelming experience. So when posts like the one my friend wrote show up on our feeds, it is so worthy of reading and reflection. We are, after all, designed for community, and sharing is such a critical part of the human experience.

Moving to the US for college and building a life here

halfway across the world from my parents meant that I was mostly around people my age, and when I was around elders, it was for social occasions and not the routine parts of daily living. There were funerals and memorials for parents of friends, but that was the formal and ceremonial part of the journey. If I could, one thing I would do differently would be to engage more broadly with people across age groups, especially those who are older, such as parents of friends. To be in the community fully means to know more closely the experience of elders. They are a wellspring of wisdom, interesting, inventive, and knowledgeable about life.

But also they can help you better understand how to show up for your own parents and even plan for your own later stages of life. Just being around that helps it become normal, helping you to be okay navigating that journey rather than avoiding or negating it. That may be a compass in itself, a tool to help you find your way to a destination in the darkness. There are people who have gone before you on the journey and developed amazing ways to guide others through challenging waters.

Recovering from an intensive period of caregiving, loss, and grief is one thing, but reinventing yourself for the longer term is a whole different thing altogether. It must be a similar experience to coming back from being at war or moving beyond a traumatic experience where everything changes—there is no going back to the old normal. That seems too far away, too unreal, and possibly not even attractive anymore. And you are changed; the old normal fit the old you and therefore cannot fit the current you. But there isn't a new you just yet. That takes time and work and patience with yourself. There isn't a road map or a path or a compass. But when you reach a new destination and can look back, you will realize that you are healing and have already come a long way.

One day, about a year after having both Mum and Dad gone, I woke up and thought, *They wanted me to be happy— how dumb of me to be anything but happy.* It was a strange moment of clarity, like a light bulb went on. From that moment, I went into a mode of seeking happiness with a vengeance. Never one to do things in half measures, I probably went a little extreme with seeking happiness, but it worked. I traveled. I joined new communities and got into coaching women on leadership. I doubled down on charitable events and building new friendships.

Meeting others who have experienced what I've been through is such a relief. Thinking you are crazy and in a parallel universe but not wanting to talk to anyone for fear they will think you crazy—that is a lonely place to be, a place full of unease and feeling unseen. But it doesn't have to be that way. At a recent dinner party, I was with a neighbor who had lost her mother tragically and young, and when someone mentioned loss we exchanged a look. *You know, you have been there,* her face told me. It was full of understanding, so powerful and affirming. Only those who have been there can get it.

We are social beings and feeling seen and understood is such a powerful driver of human emotion. When we get that affirmation, it is also healing. This is one of the main reasons for this book, as Shari and I felt this exact experience at our first meeting. We talked about our fathers and seeing them through to the end of their lives. It was so powerful that we were connected in just fifteen minutes, and thus began our book project and sharing of experiences, which has been its

own therapeutic journey of friendship and reinventing ourselves together.

SHOWING UP FOR OTHERS

One way to move forward is to show up for others as you
would want others to show up for you. We both found that we
became advocates for caregiving for our friends and colleagues
as they encountered their own challenges. Taking a supportive
role for others can be therapeutic as it helps transform your
experience into positive action for others. But it is not always
easy to do since each person is unique and can have different
needs on any given day or stage of their caregiving journey.
Here are some ways to craft your own approach to supporting
caregivers:

- Ask, and also anticipate. When Shabnam's mother
  passed away, her college roommate didn't even
  have to call and ask what she needed. She got in
  her car and drove eight hours to spend the week
  with Shabnam. This only works if you know
  someone really well and have enough experience and trust in your relationship that you can
  anticipate what they need. Otherwise, don't make
  assumptions but rather let the caregiver help you
  help them.
- Small acts of support can be as meaningful as big
  ones. A meal, a few hours to take over their active

caregiving and sit in their stead, a call or note to check in. All kinds of genuine gestures can be so appreciated.

- Sometimes all it takes is listening. Instead of attempting to fix things, give a caregiver the space to just be, talk it out, or have a break from their duties and worries. Observe, seek to understand, and be present.
- Intervene if you see things going off the rails. Both of us wish friends had pushed us to seek professional help when we were unable to function or figure out ways to self-care. It can be an uncomfortable thing to do but incredibly powerful. Like they say at airports, "If you see something, say something."
- Put yourself in their shoes. Build empathy and bring it to your actions in supporting a caregiver.

CHAPTER TAKEAWAYS

Grief is a process that takes a different amount of time for everyone. The five stages of grief are not a step-by-step manual but rather common experiences that will be uniquely experienced by each person. Take the time you need to process what you're going through, and enlist the help of family, friends, or professionals as needed. After caregiving has concluded and your loved one is gone, you have a chance to reinvent yourself: What do you want out of this next stage of life?

And now that you've been through this process, you can be a resource and beacon of light for others who are thrust into this journey. Support them however you can; we are all in this one life together.

CONCLUSION

There can be a profound sadness and grief that comes with the transition from being a child with a parent to a child parenting a parent to a child without a parent. We didn't allow ourselves much time to feel it. We are both type A people, so we threw ourselves into doer mode, making decisions, taking care of everything, staying busy. Underneath it all, though, was pain: the loss of our role as the child and the realization that things would never go back to the way they were. This was the new normal. We had to close one chapter and open another, seeing the world—and our parents—differently.

Unlike jobs, life transitions come with no training and little warning. They just happen and you have to adapt. When loved ones, especially parents, become fragile, we need to learn to see them not just for who they were but for where they are and what they need in the now. The journey unfolds before our eyes—whether we resist or not. Now is the time to embrace the transition, for everyone's sake.

Life is full of amazing steps: graduation, first jobs, babies, and other milestones. But not all milestones are fun. And there's little guidance for when you become a caregiver to your parents. It's a unique and often lonely transition, full of grief and loss. And when we pile too much on our plates, we risk burnout. The best advice is to pause, breathe, and try to be present in every moment. Find ways to fill your own cup so that you have plenty to give to everyone in your life.

As we go through caregiving for parents, it is natural to start forming a vision for our own end of life. This is excellent! It's never too early to start thinking about what you want or don't want for your own days of receiving care. Write these down or relay them to your children so you have mutual understanding. Prepare for your own final chapter and help your caregiving team be prepared.

Now that we have covered the caregiving journey from the early and middle to late stages, you can, hopefully, feel more prepared for your own journey or find ways to make adjustments to a journey already in progress. The tale of Odysseus comes to mind here—the legendary hero who faces all kinds of obstacles and trials in his ten-year journey but emerges triumphant, using his intelligence, strength, and resilience. Odysseus faces all kinds of unexpected dangers, and we learn about the human spirit from the story. His tale of perseverance and triumph is one that continues to inspire us thousands of years after it was first told because the themes and lessons are so universal.

Caregiving and the caregiving journey are not so different from *The Odyssey*. We learn from stories, we struggle against adversity, we strive to make things right and take the courageous path. And while, as caregivers, we might not feel as celebrated as Odysseus returning home, we should take pride in the endeavor—it is an ultimate challenge, and we have a chance to make a meaningful impact on those who cared for us for so many years.

As you incorporate the learnings from this book, remember that caregiving is a fundamental part of our humanity. As we serve others, we will at some point need support ourselves. If we can become wiser in our roles at each stage of caregiving, we can better inform ourselves, our children, and our families of our wishes and plans for our own end of life. Embrace the journey. Collectively, we can emerge triumphant and come home to ourselves, just like Odysseus.

References

Alzheimer's Association. "10 Steps to Approach Memory Concerns in Others." https://www.alz.org/alzheimers -dementia/10-steps.

Buettner, D. 2008. *The Blue Zones: Lessons for Living Longer from the People Who've Lived the Longest.* National Geographic.

Caring Across Generations. *Guide for Caregivers: Talking to Family, Friends, and Loved Ones About Care.* https:// caringacross.org/wp-content/uploads/2024/04/CAG -Guide-For-Caregivers.pdf.

Cobbe, T., D. Mumford, J. Mantooth, et al. 2024. *Working While Caregiving: It's Complicated.* S&P Global. https:// www.spglobal.com/en/research-insights/special-reports /working-while-caregiving.

Gawande, A. 2014. *Being Mortal: Medicine and What Matters in the End.* Metropolitan Books.

Guardian. 2023. *Standing Up and Stepping In: A Modern Look at Caregivers in the US.* https://www.guardianlife.com /reports/caregiving-in-america.

Horovitz, B. 2023. "New AARP Report Finds Family Caregivers Provide $600 Billion in Unpaid Care Across the U.S." AARP. https://www.aarp.org/caregiving/financial -legal/info-2023/unpaid-caregivers-provide-billions-in -care.html.

National Alliance for Care at Home. "Resources." https://www.caringinfo.org/resources/.

Samuels, C. 2023. "Caregiver Statistics: A Data Portrait of Family Caregiving." A Place for Mom. https://www.aplaceformom.com/senior-living-data/articles/caregiver-statistics.

Span, P. 2025. "When I Go, I'm Going Green: More Americans Are Choosing Burials in Which Everything Is Biodegradable." *New York Times*. https://www.nytimes.com/2025/08/23/health/green-natural-burials.html?unlocked_article_code=1.g08.q5av.MEMSHUKi8DFt&smid=url-share.

Statista. 2024. "Resident Population of the United States by Sex and Age as of July 1, 2023." https://www.statista.com/statistics/241488/population-of-the-us-by-sex-and-age/.

Stone, D., B. Patton, S. Heen, and R. Fisher. 2023. *Difficult Conversations: How to Discuss What Matters Most*. Penguin Publishing Group.

Van der Kolk, B. 2014. *The Body Keeps the Score: Brain, Mind, and Body in the Healing of Trauma*. Viking.

Wang, P. 2024. "How to Find a Great Home Health Aide." *Consumer Reports*. https://www.consumerreports.org/health/elder-care/how-to-find-a-great-home-health-aide-a1146419247/.

WebMD. 2024. "Burnout: Symptoms and Signs." https://www.webmd.com/mental-health/burnout-symptoms-signs.

Checklist for Eldercare Planning

PART ONE: MAKING KEY DECISIONS

PRIMARY HEALTH AND MEDICAL PLANNING

- Clarify your loved one's health status.
- Gather and review current medical conditions, diagnoses, and treatments.
- Establish a direct line of communication with all care providers.
- Review and confirm insurance coverage.
- Check which insurance plans your loved one has (Medicare, Medicaid, VA, private) and what each one covers.
- Include researching coverage for dental, vision, and any long-term care policies.
- Know the details: What does each policy pay for? What are the gaps?
- Have transparent, open, and ongoing discussions.
- Talk openly about your loved one's true health status and future needs.
- Confirm what medications they are taking and why.

- Discuss wishes for care if health worsens: Do they want care at home or in a care facility? Think through other options.
- Ask about what they want to avoid and what compromises they are willing to make.
- Identify the primary caregiver and clarify the roles of others willing to help.

LEGAL PLANNING

- Find a reputable elder law attorney familiar with your loved one's state laws.
- Obtain or ensure medical directives and power of attorney (POA) or durable POA for healthcare are in place.
- Obtain a financial POA, and make sure their will is up to date; if not, check how it can be updated depending on their health status.
- Get a good understanding of the rules around loss of capacity.

ORGANIZE FINANCIAL AFFAIRS

- Collect all financial accounts information and assess the current financial picture.
- Double-check payment setups for bills, including insurance premiums.
- Locate all accounts and assess the financial situation.

- Review all accounts, including joint accounts, and make sure they are payable upon death if you are on the account.
- Keep meticulous records of all financial transactions and budget decisions.
- If helpful, explore establishing an LLC or trust.
- Secure all passwords and access for accounts and devices—emails, phone, social media, etc.
- Consider the tax implications if you plan to claim your loved one as a dependent.

THE PLACE OF CARE

- Evaluate where your loved one will live.
- Learn about care options: staying at home, senior apartments, retirement communities, assisted living, etc.
- If you are considering senior apartments, retirement communities, or assisted living, research your options and tour facilities. Evaluate the mission of the facilities and their philosophy of care.
- Engage everyone involved in the conversations and have open discussions with your loved ones and others involved about moving, options, and other needs to make sure everyone is on the same page.
- Identify must-have amenities and services for your loved one's needs.

- Clarify costs and make sure they are transparent and you understand options for Medicare or other assisted coverage.
- Prepare for potential transitions.
- Plan for any necessary modifications to the living environment and for modifications in care.

PART TWO: THE CAREGIVING LIFE

ASSEMBLING AND MANAGING CARE

- Create a care team.
- Clarify the roles of siblings, partners, and/or extended family who will be co-caregivers.
- How does everyone feel about managing the loved one's end-of-life care?
- What are everyone's goals?
- What are everyone's fears?
- Is everyone clear about what the loved one would like?
- Establish general principles on how to share care.
- What are the skills everyone brings?
- What time commitment does everyone have?
- Who will be the primary caregiver, and how will others share and support?
- Discuss and document everything.
- What was agreed on.
- What needs to be done going forward (and who is

in charge of what).

- Information about budgets: how much is available in the loved one's assets, how much you anticipate will be needed, who will cover the gap if any.
- What choices are available, and how you will make decisions.
- What happens if there are disagreements.
- Schedule periodic check-ins.
- Understand your options for outsourcing care to professionals, or consider a hybrid model.
- Create a plan that cares for the whole person.

SELF-CAREGIVING

- Understand the signs of stress and burnout.
- Go to the doctor for regular checkups.
- Create a plan for self-care strategies—schedule time on the calendar.
- Try meditation, breathwork, or other mindfulness practices.
- Consider running, walking, yoga, or other exercise.
- Listen to others when they tell you that you need to slow down.

MANAGING CAREER AND CAREGIVING

- Understand the support program available to you

through your job. This could be an EAP, short-term or long-term disability leave, the Family and Medical Leave Act, or something else.

- Maintain open communication with your boss and colleagues.
- Evaluate whether you should stay in your job or quit.
- Can you afford to leave work? What is the state of your backup finances?
- Can you afford *not* to leave work? What is the state of your health and well-being?
- What would the off-ramping process look like?

PART THREE: FACING THE INEVITABLE AND MOVING FORWARD

END-OF-LIFE PREPARATION

- Understand the difference between hospice and palliative care, what your options are for each, and what it means to use them.
- Understand what it means to call an ambulance and for which situations that would be appropriate or not.
- Understand the different types of hospital admittance, as well as the procedures for getting a loved one checked out of the hospital.
- What is the POLST procedure like for the

hospital where your loved one is admitted?
- Spend time with your loved one, and make a plan for all interested parties to say goodbye.
- Understand the stages of death and what that may look or sound like for your loved one.

THE BUSINESS OF DEATH

- If possible, discuss with your loved one and other caregivers what their hopes and wishes are for death arrangements.
- Do they wish to be buried or cremated, or some other option?
- If they wish to be buried, where will that be? Is a plot already reserved?
- What kind of service do they want to have, and where should it take place? What details are important to them?
- Who do they wish to invite?
- Make arrangements with a funeral home.
- Choose between burial, cremation, or another path.
- Decide on caskets, urns, headstones, flowers, and other details.
- Plan the funeral or memorial service.
- Decide on the location, date, and time that work for family and loved ones.
- Consider using a funeral director to ease the decision-making process.

- Get multiple copies of the death certificate.
- Participate in death rituals, whether private or religious.

THE GRIEF PROCESS

- Understand the five stages of grief, and know that you will not move through them linearly—and that's okay.
- Reassess your responsibilities at home and with your job.
- Is there anything you can take off your plate so you can rest and recover?
- Consider getting professional help if needed.
- Show up for others who may be on a caregiving journey or going through the same thing as you.

Glossary

HOUSING TYPES

- **Aging in place:** Staying in their home with or without caregivers is growing in popularity for independent and more acute seniors.
- **Assisted living:** Assists those who may need some help with daily activities or ADLs. Has staff 24/7 and social activities; it's good to visit to make sure the residents match the health status of your loved one.
- **Continuing care retirement communities:** Offer aging in place and assisted living in one location so residents can progress through care as their needs change.
- **House sharing:** Seniors can share a home to reduce cost or live in senior apartments that only take tenants over sixty-two, but this can vary. The ownership structure of these facilities can vary between state, local, private or PE firms. Moving in with adult children is cost-effective and may require some home modifications.
- **Independent living communities:** Homes, town-homes, or apartments typically for those who

don't need assistance with their daily activities.

- **Memory care:** Specialized units, typically part of assisted living, for people with Alzheimer's disease or other forms of dementia. They are often locked facilities with staff and structured activities. Offers what is called one-to-one care.
- **Respite care:** Short-term care in an assisted living community or with skilled nursing that is intended to give primary caregivers a rest.
- **Skilled nursing:** Provides one-to-one medical care around the clock and supervision for complex or chronic conditions. Often, if an elder is in the hospital, they get released to this type of care and when/if they get stronger, they go home or to assisted living. Used to be called nursing homes and typically have long-term care as well.

OTHER TERMS

- **Durable power of attorney (POA):** A document that appoints someone you can trust to manage your financial and healthcare decisions. Requirements vary state by state, so be sure to look into this or call an attorney for help.
- **Financial abuse:** Unauthorized use of an elder's assets.
- **Hospice care:** Focuses on comfort and quality of life near the end.
- **Living will or advance directive:** A will is

often used along with a durable POA and clearly lays out the wishes of your loved one regarding healthcare so when they can't make decisions for themselves, they have a point of contact who can. A living will typically answers potential questions around feeding tubes, life support, and dialysis, and can be specific about treatments.

- **Neglect:** Failure to meet basic needs.
- **Palliative care:** Specialized medical care for serious illness.
- **POA for financial matters:** If your power of attorney is not sufficient or depending on the rules where you live, you may require more than a financial POA and may need a durable POA. It is best to consult an elder law or estate attorney where your loved one resides. This POA will designate a point of contact who will manage financial affairs when your loved one is no longer able to do so for themselves.

Acknowledgments

Shabnam

This book is dedicated to my parents, Syed Nasir Raza Kazmi and Fatiha Abbas Kazmi, for their infinite love and for teaching me everything I need to know about what truly matters. Abba and Amma, your kindness and life of giving of yourselves to others inspire me every day.

And most importantly, to my husband, Ashok; children, Zehra and Reza; and my brothers, Pervez and Ariff, who stand by my side and provide joy in moments small and large.

I also want to thank my writing partner, Shari Hofer, without whom this book would not exist. We were meant to meet and create this act of service together. I see our parents celebrating together in heaven.

Shari

To Shabnam Kazmi, my writing partner, confidant, and friend. I bet our parents are absolutely celebrating together. To my beloved husband, Jared, and our beautiful children, Beverly and Holden. You are truly the loves of my life. To my brother, Steve, my sister, Suzanne, their spouses, and my nieces and nephews.

To the YaYas, Badgers, and Beavers, thank you for always keeping me going. And to Bev and Joe Reedy, my beloved parents, whose kindness, love, and support keep me grounded, half full, and grateful every day for them.

Lastly, a huge thanks to the many friends and strangers who shared their deeply emotional stories of love, loss, and lessons in their own caregiving journeys. You are all reflected in this book, and your goodwill grows with every reader who finds comfort and help through this book.

About the Authors

Shabnam Kazmi is an accomplished biotechnology industry executive and public company board director with an MBA from Harvard Business School. She has a track record of building successful teams, businesses, and corporate alliances while at the same time championing the needs of patients and caregivers and those who are most underserved. She has received numerous awards for her public service in the nonprofit sector; she currently serves on the board of the Prevent Cancer Foundation. Shabnam is a sought-after career coach, speaker, and corporate adviser. She enjoys connecting people across continents and cultures, and finding ways to bring meaningful changes that positively impact society.

Shari Hofer is an accomplished executive and board director with more than twenty-five years of experience guiding organizations through digital, cultural, and growth transformations. Known for her authentic, people-first leadership, she has helped companies modernize operations, strengthen customer connections, and foster high-performing teams. Beyond her executive career, she mentors emerging leaders, advises start-ups, and advocates for caregivers and military families. Shari is an outdoor enthusiast; she enjoys skiing, hiking, boating, and spending time with her husband and two adult children.